Wild, Wild World of Animals

Rabbits
& Other Small Mammals

A TIME-LIFE TELEVISION BOOK

Editor: Charles Osborne
Associate Editors: Bonnie Johnson, Joan Chambers
Authors: Don Earnest, Richard Oulahan
Writers: Cecilia Waters, Deborah Heineman
Literary Research: Ellen Schachter
Text Research: Maureen Duffy Benziger
Picture Editor: Judith Greene
Permissions and Production: Cecilia Waters
Designer: Constance A. Timm
Art Assistant: Carl Van Brunt
Copy Editor: Eleanor Van Bellingham
Copy Staff: Robert Braine, Florence Tarlow

WILD, WILD WORLD OF ANIMALS
TELEVISION PROGRAM
Producers: Jonathan Donald and Lothar Wolff
This Time-Life Television Book is published by Time-Life Films, Inc.
Bruce L. Paisner, *President*
J. Nicoll Durrie, *Vice President*

THE AUTHORS

DON EARNEST was formerly a staff writer and editor with Time-Life Books. He has contributed to two previous volumes in this series, *Insects & Spiders* and *Birds of Field & Forest*, is co-author of *Life in the Coral Reef* and the author of *Songbirds* and *Life in Zoos and Preserves*.

RICHARD OULAHAN, a veteran writer, correspondent and editor for *Time, Life* and other publications of Time Inc. was text editor of the first 18 volumes of this series and the author of one, *Reptiles & Amphibians*. He is currently preoccupied with the most advanced form of animal life, as an associate editor of *People*.

THE CONSULTANT

MARY K. EVENSEN received an M.S. in zoology from the University of Minnesota. She is currently working toward her Ph.D. in biology at Queens College of The City University of New York.

COVER: A European hare takes cover amid the dense underbrush of a French forest, its brownish-gray pelage blending in with the mottled colors of the dried vegetation in which it crouches.

Wild, Wild World of Animals

Rabbits
& Other Small Mammals

Based on the television series
Wild, Wild World of Animals

Published by
TIME-LIFE FILMS

The excerpt from The Mouse from The Short Stories of Saki by H. H. Munro is reprinted by permission of The Viking Press, Inc. and The Bodley Head.

The excerpt from The Great Migrations by Georges Blond, copyright © 1956 by Macmillan Publishing Co., Inc., is reprinted by permission of Macmillan Publishing Co., Inc., and Librairie Artheme Fayard.

The excerpt from Hill Country Harvest by Hal Borland, copyright © 1967 by Hal Borland, is reprinted by permission of Carlton Knowlton Wing.

"The Chipmunk's Day," from The Bat Poet by Randall Jarrell, copyright © 1963, 1964 by Macmillan Publishing Co., Inc. is reprinted by permission of Macmillan Publishing Company and Penguin Books, Ltd.

The excerpt from Caribbean Treasure by Ivan Sanderson, copyright 1939 by Ivan T. Sanderson, is reprinted courtesy of Paul Reynolds, Inc.

ISBN 0-913948-22-5

Library of Congress Catalog Card Number: 78-62754

Printed in the United States of America.

Contents

Introduction

by Don Earnest

Man has always felt an affinity for the small mammals of the earth. Of course, the human passion to bring all creatures, especially those most nearly akin to man, into the human orbit is a basic ingredient in this feeling of closeness. But the feeling may also stem from the authentic toughness and adaptability—easily read as resourcefulness or intelligence—of many small mammals, and the response may be nurtured by a sympathetic reaction to their small size, general furriness and, in many cases, their palpable success. For whatever reason, these familiar and fascinating small creatures have been for centuries the protagonists of the oldest and most pervasive form of literary art—the folktale, with its origins in the stories told by people in every part of the world. In these stories, characters derived from small animals, like those shown in this book, have a variety of adventures that are entertaining parallels to human struggles. In many tales the wit or common sense of a vulnerable small animal overcomes the brute strength of a larger or more predatory beast. Because the rabbit is present in almost every environment, it is typical in tales from totally different cultures for the hero to be a harmless, hopping bunny, which may make that animal one of the most venerable and enduring characters in fiction.

Out of traditional folktales evolved the fable, which, though it too entertained, always ended with a moral. The inventors of fables also adopted the ubiquitous animals for their cast of characters. Among the most famous and durable of the fables are those attributed to a sixth century B.C. Greek slave known as Aesop. In his tales of foibles and failures, typical characters are the mice that make plans far too grandiose for them to carry out. Over the centuries Aesop's fables have been a favorite of children, and they are considered by many to be the ancestors of the animal stories that eventually became one of the basic components of children's fiction. Animals are featured in the popular German folktales collected and published by the brothers Grimm in the early 19th century, and they appear in the famous fairy tales of Hans Christian Andersen. But the heyday for fictional animals probably began in 1865 with the publication in England of *Alice's Adventures in Wonderland* by Lewis Carroll. Scholars have claimed that this book ushered in a golden age of children's literature, initiating a literary genre that combined stories and illustrations in imaginative and entertaining works of art. And with stories populated by the many small animals with which a child can identify, the tradition has continued up to the present day.

Thus for many English-speaking adults all over the world, Peter Rabbit; Squirrel Nutkin; Mrs. Tiggy-Winkle, the hedgehog; Mrs. Tittlemouse; and that arch villain, Samuel Whiskers, the rat, were an introduction to literature. These creatures were the creation of a remarkable woman named Beatrix Potter, whose knowledge of animals came from close observations of them in the 1870s when she was a young child from London spending summers in the country. Her earliest efforts at recording what she saw were drawings—

Literature's most famous rabbit, the White Rabbit of Lewis Carroll's Alice's Adventures in Wonderland, was drawn by John Tenniel, whose renderings of the characters are inseparable from the 1865 classic.

Samuel Whiskers

Peter Rabbit

Timmy Tiptoes

Between 1900 and 1944, Beatrix Potter wrote and illustrated 30 books for children. Her characters were small animals that children could sympathize with, such as the charming creatures on these pages.

naturalistic representations of the small wild animals and plants she encountered in the fields and meadows. Not content with merely drawing her animal subjects from a distance, by the age of 10 she was bringing home any dead specimens she could find; she skinned, boiled, dissected them and studied the skeletons. She kept mice, rabbits, hedgehogs and bats as pets, and as she grew up, her ambition was to earn a livelihood with her botanical illustrations. However, she lived in the confining Victorian age, which would not take a woman's scientific efforts seriously, and in 1900 she turned to writing and illustrating books for children. In her first book, *The Tale of Peter Rabbit,* the rabbit anatomies of Flopsy, Mopsy and Cotton-tail are absolutely correct, notwithstanding their human dress. At the time of her death in 1943, Beatrix Potter had contributed a collection of masterpieces for children that combined, in both story and illustration, realism with entrancing fantasy.

Two years after Beatrix Potter's death, a quite different kind of masterpiece was published, one that her scientifically curious mind might have relished. In 1945 the paleontologist George Gaylord Simpson published "The Principles of Classification and a Classification of Mammals," a lengthy paper that was universally acclaimed by zoologists. Drawing on his vast knowledge of fossils, in this work the author thoroughly systematized and described the orders of mammals. The small mammals in this book are classified—in accordance with the broader classifications of Simpson's system—in five major groups.

• The rabbits and the almost identical but larger hares are members of the order Lagomorpha. These long-eared hoppers share membership in their order with the pikas of North America and Eurasia.

• In contrast to the limited variety of lagomorphs, the order Rodentia, or gnawing mammals, encompasses some 1,700 of the 4,100 known species of mammals. The rodents are divided into three suborders:

The squirrels and their kin form a suborder that includes—along with more than 200 species of bushy-tailed tree climbers—ground squirrels such as chipmunks and woodchucks, and pocket gophers.

Besides mice and rats, which exist in enormous variety, the suborder of mouselike rodents comprises such diverse creatures as the tiny arboreal dormice, short-tailed voles and leaping jerboas.

The third suborder of rodents consists of the porcupine and its less prickly Central and South American relatives—cavies, agoutis, pacas, chinchillas, coypus and, an oversize oddity in an order of small animals, the capybara.

• In the order Insectivora, there are animals that are as widespread as the rabbits and rodents. Along with moles and hedgehogs, this order includes the smallest of all mammals—the shrews, some of which are no larger than a child's thumb.

• Two other major orders of mammals have members indigenous to South America. The order Marsupialia, or pouched mammals, is represented by the opossum family, with one species, the common or Virginia opossum, ranging northward into the United States, and by the ratlike caenolestids of Central America. The other order, the Edentata, contributes two disparate families: the armadillos and the tree sloths.

• Finally, Primates, the order to which man and ape belong, includes such pint-size tree dwellers as the marmoset monkeys of South America and a primitive group of creatures known as the prosimians, or pre-monkeys, which number among them the pottos and bush babies of Africa and the tarsiers of southeastern Asia.

These primates and many of the mammals that evolved in South America are restricted to tropical habitats and would probably perish in more temperate climates. They have poorly regulated body temperatures and depend on their environment for warmth. But the great majority of small mammals, typified by the familiar squirrels, hares, rats, mice, shrews and moles, are extremely adaptable animals that have successfully survived in almost every corner of the world. In part they have been able to do this because they have a high body temperature and a built-in thermostat that controls it. Together with their insulating layer of fur, this system permits them to adjust to a variety of climatic conditions. However, since their small bodies lose heat easily, many of these mammals burn energy at a much faster rate than their larger relatives and they must consume vast quantities of food to keep alive.

In addition to a high metabolic rate, there are a number of other characteristics that are shared by these small furry animals. Most of them seek out a secure haven where they can sleep, raise their young, elude predators and shelter from extremes of weather. Some build nests like the elaborate, multichambered twig structures of the dusky-footed wood rat or like the grassy balls of the European meadow mouse. Others look for ready-made homes—the abandoned tunnels of other animals, holes under rocks or roots, or hollows in logs and trees—that only need a little straw or grass for furnishing. Many dig a simple burrow. Armadillos excavate a short blind tunnel that is enlarged at the end for a nesting place; powerful diggers, they also can improvise an underground hiding place at a moment's notice. The subterranean homes of most rabbits and many rodents are also modest abodes, but for some small mammals, the construction is elaborate. The spacious accommodations of the common vole of Europe, for instance, have several chambers—with various uses—joined by a network of tunnels that includes emergency exits and passages leading to their hunting grounds.

Most small mammals are not only homemakers but also stay-at-homes that seldom venture very far from their birthplace. In experiments made by marking and then recapturing rodents, brown rats were retrieved within 40 feet of the spot where they were marked and field mice were found to have strayed no farther than a few yards. The territorial range of some mice is probably no more than a tenth of an acre, and as one study

Hunca Munca

Mouse in The Tailor of Gloucester

Benjamin Bunny

indicated, the forest deer mouse may spend its life in the area between two adjacent trees. Even the domain of some of the larger, more mobile mammals is restricted: Male cottontails have been known to stay within an area not much bigger than a city block, and females within a space half that size. The main exceptions are the small animals residing in regions where food is scarce, like the bleak tundra of the far north that is the habitat of the lemming and the arctic hare. Such small animals must travel considerable distances to obtain sufficient food.

To compensate for relatively short life spans, many small mammals are rapid breeders with young that mature very early. Although rabbits justly deserve their reputation for prolific reproduction, rats, which can have litters of 12 babies up to 10 times a year, are a good example of animals that are even more fertile. Usually the numbers of animals that can survive in a given habitat are kept in check by natural enemies, but in many parts of the world where predators have been eliminated by hunters or by loss of habitat, animal population explosions can turn the most adaptable small mammals into pests.

Most of the small mammals are fairly flexible about the food they will eat, and omnivorous feeding is the rule rather than the exception. Tree squirrels vary their diet of nuts, bark, leaves and berries with insects, eggs and even young birds. Rabbits spice their vegetarian fare with snails and grubs, porcupines are inveterate raiders of garbage dumps, and insectivorous shrews, if deprived of the enormous quantities of food they need to survive, will eat one another. But some of these tiny animals have prudently learned to survive the lean, cold months by hoarding. Gray squirrels bury caches of nuts; chipmunks and deer mice use their ample cheek pouches to transport seeds and nuts to their underground larders; and some moles lay in a store of earthworms for the winter.

The smaller mammals of the world have adapted to nearly every possible habitat. Many have taken to the trees, accommodating to an arboreal life in a variety of ways. Squirrels and marmosets use sharp claws that catch in the bark and enable them to scurry along the trunk of a tree. The claws of sedentary sloths are long, capable of hooking over a limb and allowing them to hang effortlessly, while prosimians, with opposable thumbs on their hands, clutch their perches with an almost human grasp. The coiling, prehensile tails of opossums give them an extra anchor in climbing. Some tree dwellers have effective adaptations for airborne travel as well. Bush babies have long, strong legs that permit them to bound through the foliage like bouncing balls, and flying squirrels have folds of skin stretched between their arms and legs that enable them to occasionally glide as far as 150 feet. To avoid fatal miscalculations while jumping from limb to limb and to spot food at a distance amid the foliage, most of these arboreal animals have also developed more acute eyesight than their terrestrial kin.

However, small terrestrial mammals have their own special means for surviving on solid ground, and the most amazingly efficient is the mode of locomotion called saltation, or hopping. Although this development is most often associated with rabbits and hares, other little animals are able to bound about like miniature kangaroos—a skill possessed by elephant shrews, jerboas, springhares, and the aptly named jumping mice and kangaroo rats. Whether hopping is used to search for food or to escape from predators, it—surprisingly—surpasses running as a means of covering great distances quickly. The four-inch jumping meadow mouse can cover up to 15 feet in a single leap. In its rapid, dodging mode of jumping, the kangaroo rat is able to reach a speed of 12 miles an hour. But the fastest hoppers are the rabbits and hares. Bolting away on its

snowshoe feet, the arctic hare has been clocked over a distance of three miles at slightly more than five minutes—about 35 mph.

In addition to their terrestrial and tree-climbing talents, some small mammals survive very well in the water. Most at home in its underground tunnel, the star-nosed mole is a capable swimmer when searching for food, using its wide flat arms as waterwings and its tail as a rudder; and that heavyweight rodent, the capybara, has webbed feet to help it paddle. Instead of webs, water shrews have stiff hairs between their toes, efficient enough to send them scooting across the surface of a pond. Although not specially adapted for swimming, many small mammals that live near the water, like swamp rabbits and water rats, occasionally venture into it, and even the normally arboreal and inactive sloth does a passable breaststroke.

Since his earliest beginnings, man has benefited from close and continual contact with the smaller mammals. Shrews and multitudes of other inconspicuous insect eaters have helped control the quantities of insects that otherwise would swarm over the earth; burrowers like the mole have aerated the soil and increased its arability; squirrels and other food storers, with their forgotten caches of nuts and seeds, have been prime propagators of trees and plants; and most of the small animals have always been an important source of food and fur for human populations. But aside from providing such practical gifts, which man tends to take for granted, these lesser mammals seem to strike an echoing, responsive chord in the human spirit. The power of this emotional connection is perhaps best expressed by a contemporary of Beatrix Potter's, Kenneth Grahame, acclaimed as one of the masters of English prose. Two central characters in his most celebrated book, *The Wind in the Willows*, are a mole and a water rat. In explaining why he chose to write of these lowly creatures, Grahame said it was "because I felt a duty to them as a friend. Every animal, by instinct, lives according to his nature. Thereby he lives wisely, and betters the tradition of mankind. No animal is ever tempted to belie his nature. Every animal is honest, every animal is straightforward. Every animal is true—and is, therefore, according to his nature, both beautiful and good."

Stuart Little, an adventurous mouse, is the title character of a contemporary classic created by the American writer E. B. White in 1945. The illustrator was Garth Williams.

Rabbits, Hares and Pikas

The leporids, the family of rabbits and hares, and the pikas, diminutive mountain creatures, were once classified as rodents. But today they are treated by zoologists as a separate order, the lagomorphs, a word taken from the Greek for "hare shaped."

Leporids are among the most readily identifiable of all mammals, and yet confusion reigns when it comes to distinguishing between rabbits and hares. Both have a typical bobbed tail, or scut, and eyes set on the sides of their heads, enabling them to see behind in the dangerous world in which they live. They are equipped with superb hearing, as their generally oversize ears indicate, and a keen sense of smell, which is confirmed by their comically twitching noses. In addition to such shared characteristics, the confusion between rabbits and hares is compounded by many having popular names that are misleading. The prolific jackrabbit of the western plains, for example, is actually a hare, and the Belgian hare is a true rabbit. The anatomical differences between the two are slight. In general, the up to 25-inch-long hares are larger than rabbits, which grow from eight to 14 inches long. Hares have longer legs and ears, the family's most notable characteristic. The easiest way to tell a rabbit from a hare is to observe the young: Baby rabbits, called kits or kittens, are born naked, blind and unable to move around, but newborn hares, or leverets, come into the world with open eyes and a full coat of fur, and are able to hop around like adults within a few hours after they are born.

Rabbits and hares are among the most hunted creatures on earth and are prime targets for carnivores, large birds and two-legged hunters. Prized in many parts of the world for their flesh and their soft pelts, which are often dyed and masqueraded as mink or other valuable fur, rabbits and hares have been domesticated for ages. Intensive hunting and harvesting have made them extremely nervous and alert and have cut their life expectancy to less than a year. Their survival as a species is therefore dependent on numbers, and their fecundity is no legend. A mature doe rabbit in a cold climate usually produces several litters of three to four young each year. In warm climates, where breeding goes on all year long, as many as five litters a year may be born. "Mad as a March hare" is an apt description of buck rabbits and hares during the early weeks of the spring mating season, when their leaping, gyrating courtship antics look very much like madness.

Because of their insatiable appetites for plants and bark, leporids have become a major pest in many parts of the world; notwithstanding their commercial value, they were regarded as the farmer's foe centuries before Peter Rabbit discovered Mr. McGregor's cabbage patch, in Beatrix Potter's classic children's story. They are native to nearly every continent and have adapted to nearly every climate and habitat, including deserts, swamps and the frozen tundra of northern Greenland and Alaska. Australia and New Zealand are the only sizable areas on earth where rabbits and hares are not indigenous, although they have been introduced there.

Wild hares and rabbits are such high-strung creatures, they can die of shock when they are caught. Threatened with capture or death, they squeak with fright; otherwise they spend their lives in silence, using other methods such as the warning thump of a hind foot or varying postures as means of communication.

The other lagomorphs, the pikas, are very vocal, emitting a whistling bark that they keep up almost constantly as they scurry back and forth from their dens to their forage grounds. Their high-pitched call, which has given them the name "whistling hares," serves as a warning and, for some species, as a territorial proclamation. There are 13 or 14 species of pikas that range through the highlands of Eurasia and western North America. The Old World pikas live in burrows that they dig themselves, while their New World relatives inhabit the crannies and crevices of rocky mountaintops.

Pikas are smaller than the smallest rabbits, never growing more than eight inches long. With their tiny, rounded ears they look much more like guinea pigs than like the other leporids. And they are extremely resourceful. Pikas build miniature haystacks of vegetation as provender against the winters when mountains are covered with snow. The haystacks are portable, and the pikas carry them into their rock crevices at night and in rainy weather and drag them out to dry in the sunshine.

Pikas are not nearly as prolific as other lagomorphs. A female may produce two litters a year in spring and summer, and the two to five young are born with eyes and ears closed. By the time of the first frost of their first autumn, however, the young pikas are independent and busily assembling their own haystacks to tide them over the long winter months.

Black-tailed jackrabbit

The Cottontail Clan

With its sassy white scut, the cottontail rabbit is the prototype for every storybook rabbit, from Alice's guide through Wonderland to Uncle Remus' Br'er Rabbit. All cottontails look pretty much alike and are instantly identifiable by their powder-puff tails. North American cottontails make their homes in holes abandoned by other animals, in dense underbrush, briar patches or any convenient clump of tall grass. The common rabbit of Europe, the ancestor of many varieties of rabbits, is also a cottontail and is virtually indistinguishable from its New World cousins, but its housing arrangements are quite distinctive. Almost unique among leporids, the European rabbits are true burrowers that dig vast underground warrens. The focal point of this subterranean network is the chamber of the queen doe and king buck, whose daughters, sons, grandchildren and more remote descendants occupy the surrounding interconnected holes. Members of the most recent generation are relegated to the outermost perimeters of the warren in the holes that are most vulnerable to weasels, foxes and other invading predators.

The cottontail of the arid flatlands of the western U.S. desert and the Mexican altiplano (right), is slightly more slender and harelike in appearance than other members of the family. When threatened, cottontails will often freeze, and they can hold a motionless posture for five minutes or more.

The familiar cottontail of eastern North America (below) beds down in tall grasses during the heat of the day, becoming most active in the early morning and at sundown. Cottontails have a Jekyll and Hyde reputation: They are the delight of hunters, as game animals, and the despair of farmers, as a serious menace to crops.

Scampering through a frozen cornfield (left), a cottontail is an easy mark for predators. As the weather turns cold, their color does not change like that of their relatives, the larger northern hares.

Dried cornstalks form a windbreak for a cottontail (above). In winter, rabbits usually seek a more sheltered nest than in summer. During severe weather they may huddle in their shelters for days, but they never hibernate.

Bunny Mothers

The cottontail rabbit's reputation for prolific reproduction is well earned. In the course of a year, a cottontail doe generally will bear several litters, each averaging four or five young. Shortly after she has given birth, the North American cottontail doe leaves her naked, blind and helpless young in a shallow depression that she has scooped out of the ground and lined with grass and soft fur from her underbelly. She covers the litter with a blanket of grass, which provides camouflage and warmth as she forages nearby. At dawn and dusk, the doe returns to squat over the nest and nurse the hungry babies. When the kits are able to move around, the mother may simply sit upright by the nest at feeding time and let the youngsters come to her.

Because they build their nests at the edges of fields, golf courses and other man-made clearings, New World cottontails are often the victims of threshers or lawn mowers. The young of European cottontails, born in underground burrows, have more secure infancies, but when they are about four weeks old, like all cottontails, they leave the nest and hop off into a hazardous world.

Young European cottontails huddle together instinctively when the cover of their nursery burrow is removed (right). Two American cottontail nestlings (bottom right) are fully furred, and soon will be ready to leave the nest.

A European cottontail doe watches as her young offspring leaves the safety of its burrow (below). At this point the kit's life expectancy is less than one year, but if it manages to survive that critical period, the chance of its living to the ripe old age of two years is vastly increased.

Jackrabbit Marauders

There is no sign of them during the burning daylight hours on the western plains except for millions of telltale footprints in the dust. But with the approach of darkness, the jackrabbits emerge, in astonishing hordes that fill the landscape, to forage through the night. Largest of the lagomorphs, jackrabbits are actually hares. If their smaller cousins, the true rabbits, are regarded as truck-garden nuisances, the jackrabbits must be classified as marauders of the plains. Numbering in the millions, their depredations of grazing lands are a major problem for cattle and sheep breeders. It has been estimated that in a single day, 30 jackrabbits consume as much as a large sheep does and that 128 jackrabbits can match a cow in the daily consumption of grass. Domestic crops, such as alfalfa, soybeans, cabbage and clover, make up a good part of the jackrabbit's diet, at least during the summer. In the winter, when these foods are unavailable, the menu changes to include twigs, bark, dried grass and roots.

Efforts to control the jackrabbit population have been frustrated by the animal's wily instinct for survival. Poisons have proved ineffective. Pursued, they race in a confusing, broken-field pattern at speeds of up to 35 mph and are able to dodge most natural predators. Their springing leaps normally cover as much as 10 feet, and when they are startled the big jacks can bound twice that distance, changing direction as they fly through the air.

24

One of the largest hares, the white-tailed
jackrabbit (above) is distinguished by its tail,
which remains white throughout the year.
Its coat changes with the seasons, from
gray-brown in summer to pearl-gray or
white in winter.

Outlandish ears and pale coloration mark the
long-legged antelope jackrabbit (opposite), a
familiar denizen of the U.S. Southwest. A hardy
survivor in its desert habitat, it eats almost any
available vegetation, including cacti.

The black-tailed jackrabbit (right) is the
archetypal hare of the American West, branded
by cattlemen and sheepherders as the No. 1
"varmint." Black tips on its oversize ears and
a black streak down its tail distinguish it
from other jackrabbits.

Hair of the Hare

In *The Eve of Saint Agnes*, the poet John Keats wrote what have been called the coldest lines in English verse: "The owl, for all his feathers, was a-cold; The hare limp'd trembling through the frozen grass." But Keats could never have meant the snowshoe, or varying, hare: Not one of these hardy lagomorphs of the New World's northern regions would limp, even in the coldest weather, unless it was wounded or afflicted with disease.

The snowshoes and their close kin, the Arctic and tundra hares, are wonderfully adapted to their far northern habitats. Their huge rear feet are padded with short, dense hair that permits them to scamper across the thinnest snow crusts or to bound like kangaroos across the icy wastelands. The front paws of the Arctic hare are equipped with very sharp claws that can penetrate the ice and snow to locate tender roots and bark underneath, which the hares pull up with their pincerlike front teeth. In winter, the northern hares are camouflaged in fine, snow-white outer coats of guard hairs overlying a layer of thick, warm underfur. As the short northern summer approaches, these winter coats are gradually shed, to be replaced by lightweight gray or brown summer pelages.

In its winter coat (above) the snowshoe hare has pure white guard hairs that cover a thick, windproof coat of yellowish fur. In extremely bitter weather, though, the hares tunnel under the ice crust, where they wait out the severest storms.

The snowshoe hare's between-seasons coat is a patchwork of white and brown (top, right), which accounts for its other common name: varying hare. In time, the snowshoe dons its summer camouflage of dark brown (right).

A bobcat stalks and kills a cottontail in deep snow (sequence above and at left). Rabbits and hares, as well as rodents of all kinds, are the principal items of the bobcat's diet.

A red-tailed hawk (opposite, top), has just felled a rabbit but not yet killed it. Whether the bird will be able to carry off its relatively large victim is dubious. The red fox (opposite, bottom) has no such problem, as it jauntily makes off with a fat cottontail.

Enemies List

Rabbits and hares are a major link in the food chain. They consume vegetable matter that is converted to flesh, which then provides one of the principal foods of many predators. As a consequence, the "enemies list" of rabbits includes almost any carnivorous mammal that crosses their path, from weasels and foxes to the big cats, as well as large snakes and most birds of prey. The largest of such birds, like the golden eagle, are able to carry off an adult rabbit or hare after they have made the kill; smaller raptors, including hawks, consume their prey on the ground, often leaving scraps for such carrion-eating birds as buzzards, crows and ravens.

"First catch one hare" is the instruction in an ancient recipe for jugged hare, but this is easier said than done. With their great agility, speed and nervous wariness, leporids are hard to catch. As a result, predators usually manage to kill only the old, sick or very young, and actually perform a kind of ecological service by culling from the rabbit population all but the fittest members, indirectly helping to keep the species strong and healthy.

Wildlife Near Home

by Dallas Lore Sharp

Rabbits in the wild are wary animals whose daily activities are not easily witnessed by man. In Wildlife Near Home, *excerpted below, Dallas Lore Sharp, a compassionate observer of small animals, allows us to be uninvited guests as a group of New England rabbits indulge in a moment of pure frivolity.*

At one time my home was separated from the woods by only a clover-field. This clover-field was a favorite feeding-ground for the rabbits of the vicinity. Here, in the early evening, they would gather to feed and frolic; and, not content with clover, they sometimes went into the garden for a dessert of growing corn and young cabbage.

Take a moonlight night in autumn and hide in the edge of these woods. There is to be a rabbit party in the clover-field. The grass has long been cut and the field is clean and shining; but still there is plenty to eat. The rabbits from both sides of the woods are coming. The full moon rises above the trees, and the cottontails start over. Now, of course, they use the paths which they cut so carefully the longest possible way round. They hop leisurely along, stopping now and then to nibble the sassafras bark or to get a bit of wintergreen, even quitting the path, here and there, for a berry or a bunch of sweet wood-grass.

"Stop a moment; this won't do! Here is a side-path where the briers have grown three inches since they were last cut off. This path must be cleared out at once," and the old buck falls to cutting. By the time he has finished the path a dozen rabbits have assembled in the clover-field. When he appears there is a *thump,* and all look up; some one runs to greet the new-comer; they touch whiskers and smell, then turn to their eating.

The feast is finished, and the games are on. Four or five rabbits have come together for a turn at hop-skip-and-jump. And such hop-skip-and-jump! They are professionals at this sport, every one of them. There is not a rabbit in the game that cannot leap five times higher than he can reach on his tiptoes, and hop a clean ten feet.

Over and over they go, bounding and bouncing, snapping from their marvelous hind legs as if shot from a spring-trap. It is the greatest jumping exhibition that you will ever see. To have such legs as these is the next best thing to having wings.

Right in the thick of the fun sounds a sharp *thump! thump!* Every rabbit "freezes." It is the stamp of an old buck, the call, *Danger! danger!* He has heard a twig break in the woods, or has seen a soft, shadowy thing cross the moon.

As motionless as stumps squat the rabbits, stiff with the tenseness of every ready muscle. They listen. But it was only a dropping nut or a restless bird; and the play continues.

They are chasing each other over the grass in a game of tag. There go two, round and round, tagging and re-tagging, first one being "it" and then the other. Their circle widens all the time and draws nearer to the woods. This time round they will touch the bush behind which we are watching. Here they come—there they go; they will leap the log yonder. Flash! squeak! scurry; Not a rabbit in the field! Yes; one rabbit—the limp, lifeless one hanging over the neck of that fox trotting off yonder in the shadows, along the border of the woods!

The picnic is over for this night, and it will be some time before the cottontails so far forget themselves as to play in this place again.

It is small wonder that animals do not laugh. They have so little play. The savage seldom laughs, for he hunts and is hunted like a wild animal, and is allowed so scant opportunity to be off guard that he cannot develop the power to laugh. Much more is this true of the animals. From the day an animal is born, instinct and training are bent toward the circumvention of enemies. There is no time to play, no chance, no cause for laughter.

The little brown rabbit has least reason of all to be glad. He is utterly inoffensive, the enemy of none, but the victim of many. Before he knows his mother he understands the meaning of *Be ready! Watch!* He drinks these words in with his milk. The winds whisper them; the birds call them; every leaf, every twig, every shadow and sound, says: *Be ready! Watch!* Life is but a series of escapes, little else than vigilance and flight. He must sleep with eyes open, feed with ears up, move with muffled feet, and, at short stages, he must stop, rise on his long hind legs, and listen and look. If he ever forgets, if he pauses one moment for a wordless, noiseless game with his fellows, he dies. For safety's sake he lives alone; but even a rabbit has fits of sociability, and gives way at times to his feelings. The owl and the fox know this, and they watch the open glades and field-edges. They must surprise him.

Forever processing its food for the winter months, a pika gathers grasses, thistles and other mountain greenery for its "haystack" (left). A collared pika (left, below) takes the summer sun in Alaska in a rare respite from the constant chore of assembling its stack.

The Whistlers

The smallest, least-known and perhaps most appealing lagomorphs are the pikas, industrious seven-inch-long creatures that whistle while they work and, for the most part, keep wisely out of the sight of humans. Most New World pikas live in the crevices of rockslides in the mountains of western North America; some of their Asiatic cousins dig burrows. Like many other small animals of northern latitudes, pikas spend most of their time gathering food to last them through the long winter, when they may be confined for weeks under the blanketing snow. They are unsociable, yet they choose to live in aggregations, with each male fiercely defending his own tiny territory. Pikas communicate warning signals to each other night and day in whistles so piercing that they nearly drive campers in the high Sierras out of their minds.

A fat-cat grain merchant if ever there was one, a pika stands in front of its summer harvest of grasses, neatly stowed under a boulder (below). Winter provender is not shared with the family, and the summer's offspring must begin making their haystacks when only a few weeks old.

Opossums

Whether ambling along the ground with its slow rolling gait, or climbing through the trees at night with a dozen jiggling babies on its back, the opossum has always appeared in popular North American legend as different from other animals. The difference, in fact, is substantial: The opossum is not only the sole representative of the marsupial order in North America but also the member of the marsupial family that has diverged the least from its original ancestors and is the most primitive mammal in North America. Opossums, and all other marsupials, are distinguished from other mammals by bearing their young in an embryonic state and nurturing them from mammary glands within a pouch or under folds in the mother's skin. Outside Australia and nearby islands, where marsupials from the kangaroo to the koala have diversified and flourished, the only existing marsupials are two American families: a small group called Caenolestidae, which consists of the rat opossums, and the abundant opossum family, or Didelphidae.

The familiar folktale opossum of North America, known as the Virginia, or common, opossum, migrated northward from South America in fairly recent times, leaving behind two close relatives that differ in having darker coloration and shorter fur but are similar in general appearance. Since its range now extends from Argentina to southern Canada, the Virginia opossum can be considered the most adaptable—and certainly the most widespread—member of the family.

Equipped like most primitive marsupials with a clawless opposable toe on each hind foot, a naked prehensile tail and elongated snout, this northern opossum has prospered for many reasons. It is basically a shy animal and a solitary nomad that moves about under cover of darkness. Often spending as much time in trees as on the ground, it is a skilled climber, able to coil its long tail tightly around a branch. And although the opossum can hang from its tail, it most often makes use of this appendage to ease itself from one limb to another.

Despite its affinity for trees, the opossum usually seeks residence in relatively open terrain—at the forest's edge, in a swamp or thicket-covered wasteland. It ranges over an area of from 15 to 40 acres, gathering dried grass for a nest with its prehensile tail. After a night of quiet prowling, sometimes covering two or three miles, it settles down in the hollow of a log or under a brush heap. Over the years the opossum has adapted well to farmlands and even to parks in suburbs and cities. Any place is suitable if it can easily find water.

Opossums are equally adaptable in their feeding habits, changing their diet with the season and terrain. They are essentially scavengers and will eat almost anything, dead or alive—insects, snakes, birds and small mammals such as mice and moles. In season they gorge on fruit, and in the southern United States they are known to have a special fondness for pokeberries and persimmons. Opossums are meticulous about cleaning themselves, industriously licking their fur and combing it with their paws while balancing on their hind legs and tail.

Opossums themselves are part of the diet of many larger, more aggressive creatures, including foxes, wolves, dogs, cats, hawks, owls—and man, who values their fur and porklike flesh. But an opossum often is able to outsmart its predators with its unique mode of defense—the death-feigning act that contributed the phrase "playing possum" to the language. Essentially a desperate maneuver that is used only when there is no other escape, the opossum's imitation of having departed this world is one of the most convincing charades in the animal kingdom. This skillful actor not only collapses in a limp heap but also has its eyes tightly shut, its tongue lolling from a partially open mouth and its teeth bared in a macabre grimace. And it can be prodded, kicked, picked up and dropped without any response that would reveal its ruse. After a few sniffs, most predators leave the opossum, which quickly resumes its normal routine.

The smaller South and Central American members of the family Didelphidae do not share the North American opossums' acting ability. But like their cousins in North America, these tropical marsupials have adapted extremely well to a variety of habitats. The yapok, or water opossum, is aquatic, the only marsupial that can be so considered; the shrew opossum lives under loose soil; and the rat-size woolly opossum and the four-eyed opossum are tree dwellers. Probably the most numerous of these southern opossums is the minuscule murine opossum, which is common on the edge of forests and on banana plantations from Mexico to Panama. Occasionally one of these creatures puts in an unexpected appearance in the United States when, to the consternation of shoppers and store owners, it emerges from a bunch of bananas.

Pockets Full of Possums

Opossums have existed since the age of dinosaurs 200 million years ago, and these marsupials are still primitive mammals, not far removed by evolution from their ancestral stock. The hardy opossums have a range that extends from South to North America; they have ventured as far north as Canada, adapting to differing climatic conditions and adjusting their diet accordingly. They reproduce frequently and abundantly, but no more than 13 offspring will survive out of a litter of as many as 20. This attrition is the result of an odd disparity: The female has only 13 teats from which to suckle; therefore only the firstborn or the strongest individuals to reach the pouch, after a journey from the birth canal across the mother's belly, have a chance to live. These embryonic opossums, smaller than honeybees, attach themselves to the mammary glands and remain there for up to three months. At that time they will be sufficiently developed to leave the pouch for short periods, and, particularly when the pouch becomes too crowded, some of the babies will begin clinging to the mother's back. Although opossums are flexible in feeding and are at home in trees, in water or on the ground, they have a short life span, rarely living more than two years.

Still under strict maternal supervision, these seven-week-old opossums (opposite) will not be mature enough to leave their mother for about six more weeks. In the picture above, one youngster rides piggyback while its sibling makes a less successful attempt to climb aboard its mother's back.

A 10-week-old opossum (right) has climbed out of its mother's pouch—its initial move toward independence. Several weeks later it will face the prospect of foraging for its own food and building a well-camouflaged and comfortable nest. If it survives, it will start its own family within a year or so.

An opossum paddles proficiently through a waterway in Georgia's Okefenokee Swamp. Though basically a terrestrial mammal, the opossum, with its opposable hind toes, long claws on its forefeet, and prehensile tail, is also adapted for climbing in trees.

With its 50 sharp teeth the opossum can be a creature to be reckoned with. Although it is not aggressive, usually preferring retreat rather than confrontation, if it is strongly provoked, it may turn on its attacker and deliver a painful bite.

When cornered, an opossum often plays dead, rolling over onto its side to assume a limp, comatose posture. It will not stir until it is sure that the danger is past.

Insectivores

Tiny energetic shrews, dim-sighted tunneling moles, prickly hedgehogs and shaggy solenodons may seem an oddly diverse group to belong to the same category of the animal kingdom. Yet all are members of an ancient, very successful order of small ground-dwelling mammals known as Insectivora. As the name implies, these animals primarily eat insects, but they also consume worms, snails, centipedes, crustaceans and any number of other small creeping and crawling creatures that venture within range of their long, ceaselessly probing snouts. And when invertebrates are in short supply, insectivores will also nibble on grass, seeds, bulbs and other vegetable matter. As a matter of fact, life is a nearly continuous round of eating for many insectivores, which have extremely rapid metabolic processes for converting food to energy and tissue and are thus among the most ravenous animals in the world.

The peak of prodigious consumption is reached by the omnivorous shrews. The more voracious of these restless, irascible little creatures can consume the equivalent of their own body weight in three or four hours of fast and furious feasting. The most numerous family of the insectivores, shrews are found in fields, woodlands, marshes and even suburban backyards and city parks throughout the world, except in Australia and most of South America. But few people ever see them because they spend so much of their lives under cover—scurrying through brush and leaf litter, scooting through tunnels often dug by other animals and burrowing into their own nests. At first sight, shrews are often mistaken for mice, and they do look very much like those ubiquitous rodents, although they have longer, sharper snouts, smaller ears and more streamlined bodies —all adaptations well suited to a career spent searching in and out of nooks and crannies for food.

One reason for the shrews' high metabolism is their small size, which causes them to lose body heat more quickly than larger animals do. Indeed, two minute members of the shrew family can probably lay equal claim to the title of world's smallest mammal: Both the pygmy shrew of North America and the Etruscan shrew of Italy weigh about a tenth of an ounce. The ribs of these mammalian mites are not much thicker than a bristle, and it would take almost 200 of these shrews to register a pound on the scale.

The shrew's subterranean cousin, the mole, is most remarkable for a body totally specialized for tunneling through the earth. The most outstanding adaptation is the functional form of the forelimbs, which have evolved as enormous clawed scoops that plow through the loose moist loam of meadows, lawns and forest floors with a motion like that of a swimmer. Leaving its characteristic trail— meandering ridges of cracked earth or untidy heaps of dirt known as molehills—the eastern mole of North America excavates at the rate of one foot a minute. When frost forces it to move down into harder subsoil, this indefatigable miner can still proceed at 15 feet an hour. Like the shrew, the mole is driven by an insatiable appetite, and its daily food intake, although somewhat more modest than a shrew's, is still often equal to its weight.

Moles do have eyes, but they are vestigial organs only able to distinguish between light and dark. Moles are nevertheless able to navigate rapidly and easily through their dark subterranean world, using their highly developed senses of hearing and touch—their tactile noses have thousands of sensitive nerve endings at the tip. One of these underground dwellers, the star-nosed mole, even has a fringe of pink tentacles around the end of its snout that serve as feelers.

Despite their inconspicuous life-styles, the common mole and shrew have been familiar enough over the ages for humans to have appropriated their names for epithets—the "mole" working in the dark and the "shrew" of difficult disposition. But among the insectivores are more unusual creatures, such as the elephant shrews of Africa and the rare solenodons of Haiti and Cuba. Solenodons, the most threatened of the insectivores, have impressive defenses: strong, sharp teeth and a secretion of venomous saliva. However, these weapons have not saved the 20-inch-long animal from the predations of the islands' introduced populations of cats, dogs and mongooses, and its numbers are rapidly diminishing.

While moles find protection in their subterrestrial tunnels, and shrews in their undercover agility and aggressiveness, their relative, the hedgehog, which forages openly in the forests of Europe and parts of Asia and Africa, has survived by being a walking bramble. From its forehead to the base of its tail, the hedgehog is covered by a thick growth of short, stiff spines tipped with needle-sharp points. And this formidable defense is complemented by a unique muscular reflex in the presence of danger: The threatened hedgehog can roll its body into a prickly round package that is practically impossible to open.

Untamable Shrews

The shrew family consists of almost 300 species that require from their habitat only moisture—and a supply of food sufficient for their insatiable appetites. These hyperactive animals, which may starve if they go without food for several hours, lead solitary and secretive lives, communicating with each other when necessary by rapid, high-pitched squeaks. Although their eyesight is poor, their senses of smell and touch are excellent, and they are often aided in their constant quest for food by sensitive hairs around their tactile snouts. Shrews consume quantities of insects, but they will eat anything they can manage to kill, often victimizing voles and mice that are the same size as themselves.

Even if a shrew is not caught by one of its predators, such as an owl or weasel, its normal life-span is only about a year and a half. But in this brief period it matures, and it breeds as often as three times, having as many as seven offspring in a litter. The minuscule babies are born with permanent teeth, and in response to danger the young of some species will trail in a line after their mother, each baby fastening firmly with its teeth onto the rump of the one in front.

A musk shrew (above) leans against a termite mound in West Africa, sniffing with its sensitive snout for a meal. Glands under the skin of musk shrews produce an unpleasant smell. These voracious animals effectively control insects, including household pests.

A pair of East African long-eared elephant shrews (left) peer down their long, mobile noses. Elephant shrews are not true shrews but members of a separate insectivore family. Unlike shrews, these large-eyed animals are gentle, give birth to two young at a time and pursue large ants for food.

Plump and splay-footed, a northern water shrew rests on a rock above a creek in Colorado. This dim-sighted swimming shrew has stiff hairs on its hind feet that help propel it through the water. The long hairs surrounding its snout serve as antennae for locating prey.

A northern water shrew (below) chews a grasshopper. Although insects are a major item in the water shrew's diet, it often feeds on snails, and occasionally this semiaquatic animal, which is capable of staying underwater for several seconds, dives after a small fish.

A two-inch California desert shrew (right) begins ingesting a centipede. The teeth of a shrew function somewhat like pincers, chopping up prey piece by piece until every bit is swallowed. This apparently substantial centipede meal will only satisfy the desert shrew for a few hours.

A short-tailed shrew (above) feeds on a vole it has killed. After this four-inch shrew has punctured its victim with its teeth, poisonous saliva is secreted into the wound, paralyzing the prey so it can be eaten at leisure.

A star-nosed mole (left) seeks out worms on the earth's surface, where this mole spends some of its time. It also is capable of digging deep under the mud of its marshy habitat, and frequently swims. The 22 tentacles on the snout of the star-nosed mole (right) are an additional adaptation for the weak-eyed animal, which relies mainly on its sense of touch both underground and underwater.

The five-fingered paddlelike hand of a starnose (right) is broader than it is long and contributes to the starnose's swimming ability as well as furnishing an efficient excavating tool.

An eastern mole (right) emerges from its tunnel. Its prominent splayed-out forelimbs operate like strong scoops to throw earth behind it. When the ground freezes in the eastern mole's habitat, it digs through the hard earth to reach a pre-excavated burrow in which it spends the winter below the frost line.

Mole Mobility

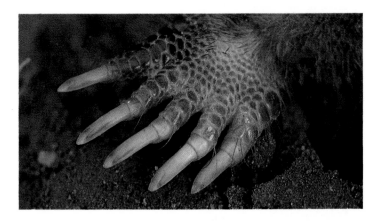

The moles, with representatives in Europe, Asia and North America, exhibit more variety in anatomy than the similarly energetic shrews. A prime example is the star-nosed mole of North America, which has a fringe of mobile, tactile tentacles surrounding its nose. A special piece of sensory equipment, the animal's bizarre-looking nose helps it to locate worms, leeches and insects both on land and in the water—despite its nearly total blindness.

The eyes of all moles are extremely weak, and in some species the eyes are completely covered with skin. Most moles have sensory hairs on their feet, and hearing that can perceive the slightest vibration in their subterranean environment. Besides the fine sense of touch supplied by the naked nose, the organ also functions as an extra earth-moving appendage. For burrowing, moles have broad, powerful forelimbs equipped with long claws that enable them to dig swiftly and untiringly, either just under the surface of the ground, as the eastern mole usually does, or straight down—in seconds—to considerable depth. It is possible for the mole to change course easily in the close quarters of a narrow tunnel by making turns that resemble a half somersault.

Fearless and Harmless

The hedgehog, a native of Europe with relatives in Asia and Africa, has almost nothing to fear. Its back is covered with spines from forehead to tail, and although the spines are less than an inch long, unbarbed and nondetachable, the hedgehog can erect them at the slightest whiff of danger, converting itself into an unpalatable ball. Supplementing this prickly armor is a kind of immunity: A hedgehog has a high degree of resistance to poisons from the bites of snakes and the stings of wasps and bees, and even to noxious man-made chemicals. With these protective devices, the amiable hedgehog, unlike the retiring shrews and moles, wanders openly aboveground in a variety of habitats, from its preferred woodlands to fields and gardens.

Hedgehogs are omnivorous and seem limited in what they eat only by the small size of their mouths. Using their sense of smell, they forage for fruits, vegetables, insects, slugs and snails. At the onset of winter, the hedgehog withdraws into a nest of vegetation and hibernates until warmer weather restores a food supply to its habitat.

The placid behavior of the hedgehog takes a lively turn during courtship. The male initiates a butting battle with a female, banging his forehead, with spines erect, against hers. After a while she begins to butt back, and the sparring may go on for hours. Breeding occurs twice a year, producing four to five blind and naked young that will not reach maturity for seven months.

Transformed into a round thicket of prickles (left), a hedgehog presents an unappetizing appearance to any predator. A muscle structure in its skin operates like a drawstring, encircling the hedgehog's body and enabling it to draw itself into a ball with its vulnerable snout and belly tucked in.

A hedgehog cranes toward its back (below) in a routine washing of its spines with saliva. Besides this frequent, regular grooming, any strong smell—including that of an unfamiliar hedgehog—will stimulate it to take a spit bath.

Encountering a viper (left), a hedgehog erects its spines to avoid penetration by the fangs. However, the hedgehog is resistant to snake venom and occasionally will feed on a viper.

In typical solitude, a hedgehog ambles confidently across a stream on its thin, short legs (left). Hedgehogs are mostly active in the early morning or evening, and despite their ungainly appearance, they are good swimmers and able to climb rocks and trees.

A hibernating hedgehog (above) is in such torpor that it can be turned undisturbed onto its back. Hedgehogs eat heavily before cold temperatures trigger sleep and, curled under a blanket of leaves, survive on stored fat.

50

A quartet of young hedgehogs (below) sniffs its surroundings. Smell is a hedgehog's most important sense for locating food. By six weeks, young hedgehogs have developed an efficient coat of spines, but for several more months they will follow their mother on feeding forays.

Primates

Amid the foliage of the earth's great tropical forests, a number of diminutive primates, members of the same order of mammals that includes man and the great apes, have adapted to an almost totally tree-bound existence. Some of these small primates are monkeys from the least sophisticated stratum of the anthropoid world. Many, however, belong to an even more primitive group of primates known as the prosimians, or pre-monkeys.

Although prosimians have retained many primitive characteristics, they also have advanced sensory and motor skills that make them efficient nocturnal and arboreal animals. Some of their senses are highly developed. Their eyes, which are unusually large in proportion to their skulls, are set close to the center of their faces, giving them the visual depth perception that is necessary for moving about in the trees without falling. They have dexterous fingers and toes, and most prosimians' thumbs and big toes are opposed to the other digits, allowing them to grip a branch firmly. Instead of claws, they have nails on all their digits but one, which make their hands appear extremely human. (The claw on a single toe is for grooming and scratching themselves.)

Among the most successful and abundant of these prosimians are the galagos, which are found in most of the forested regions of Africa. The smallest of these creatures is only the size of a mouse. Galagos are wide eyed and long tailed, and they have soft, woolly fur and large, mobile ears. Because their call sounds like the cry of a human infant, they are popularly known as bush babies. Gregarious and nocturnal animals, they huddle together when they settle down in a tree hollow after an active night of foraging, which they do either singly or in pairs. They are superb acrobats capable of virtuoso leaps of up to seven feet. Using their long, well-developed hind legs, bush babies bound from branch to branch with agility and accuracy. They fly unharmed through thickets of vines and branches and they sometimes shoot through the air almost too fast for the human eye to follow.

Another accomplished prosimian acrobat is the tarsier, which lives in the rain forests of Malaysia, Indonesia and the Philippines. With its special jumper's legs—lengthy limbs that are further elongated by having extended ankle bones—this animal is a skillful gymnast. The tarsier can reverse direction in midair, and it has disk-shaped pads on its fingers and toes that enable it to cling to smooth, vertical surfaces. As if these athletic attributes were not enough, the limber tarsier can swivel its head around to look behind its own back.

Other prosimians, however, are almost as slow in their movements as the bush babies and tarsiers are agile. One is the potto of Central Africa, a woolly, rotund member of the loris family, that looks like a small bear. The potto is a careful and deliberate tree climber. Alternating arms and legs, and moving hand over hand, sometimes on top of a branch and sometimes under it, it sneaks up on the insects and birds it preys upon. But despite its cautious ways, the potto can react quickly enough if necessary, and it is an able climber with a grip so strong that it cannot be pulled off a branch even when it is asleep. One West African potto, the angwantibo, or golden potto, is a skillful if slow-motion tumbler: It can turn a somersault by walking its front legs back between its hind legs.

Even smaller than most prosimians is a singular family of New World monkeys that includes the marmosets and the similar tamarins. In many ways these monkeys, which are mostly rat-size and have squirrel-like habits, are more primitive than other simians—and even more than some prosimians. Because they depend on claws that hook their lightweight bodies onto the bark when they scamper in the treetops, they have not developed the specialized limbs and firm grip possessed by the leaping and swinging prosimians and by other monkeys. However, they have attributes that seem to compensate.

The family name, Callithricidae, derives from the Greek for "beautifully haired," and marmosets may be maned, moustached or topknotted. Their variety of hairdos is matched by their gamut of facial expressions and by the complexity of communication that is suggested in their myriad birdlike vocalizations. Marmosets live in family units as do many other primates, but with one unusual difference. Unlike most primates, the father takes care of the young, usually twins and sometimes triplets, giving them to his mate only when they need to be suckled. And he will carry the burden of babies on his back until their total weight is almost equal to his own.

Baby-sitting marmoset fathers of the pygmy species, probably the smallest living primates, must cope with incredibly tiny young. Newborn pygmy marmosets, although fully furred and formed, are so small that a magnifying glass is needed to see their fingers.

A limber bush baby (above) executes an adroit body twist
worthy of the most skillful contortionist. This galago
enjoys a reputation as the acrobat of the loris group. Its
basic repertoire features many spectacular tree-to-tree
leaps through the upper branches.

54

A Show of Hands

Among the order of primates, even the least evolved—such as those shown on these pages—have manual and acrobatic skills that are the equal of those possessed by more sophisticated members of the group. A case in point is the nocturnal mouse lemur, a prosimian that lives only on the island of Madagascar. It has very well-developed hands. The elongated fingers wrap around the delicate branches in the very tops of the forest tree canopy, where it finds its niche, and the five-inch lemur makes its way through the leafy maze with great finesse.

The West African potto, a loris, has one of the most perfectly adapted systems of opposable digits in the primate world: The hand has a vestigial stump instead of an index finger, so it is the thumb and third finger that are opposable. This unusual adaptation heightens the grasping ability of the potto and its grip is sure and steady.

The dwarf galago—or bush baby—of southern and eastern Africa, deals with the challenges of its habitat with a more dazzling athletic flair than most of its loris relatives. Leaping through the treetops with unerring precision, it depends on its acute eyesight, abundant energy and surefootedness for its unfailingly perfect landings.

Life in the tall trees of the Madagascan rain forests—where a misstep means a long and possibly fatal drop—produced specialized adaptations in mouse lemurs. Four of the agile prosimians (right) show off the tree-climbing prowess they have developed in response to the challenge.

A potto (opposite), climbing with care into a tree, wraps its well-articulated fingers around a slender branch to get a firm grip. Although the potto is slow moving, it can successfully negotiate its way to the treetops.

Poised for a sudden thrust upward by its long, sturdy legs, the bush-tailed galago above is ready to launch itself on one of its dramatic jumps. The galago's thick, fleshy toe pads help it absorb the shock of a sudden landing.

Minute Simians

Marmosets, exotic-looking natives of the tropical rain forests of Central and South America, are among the smallest primates: The largest species measure under 15 inches in length, excluding their long, slender tails. The pygmy marmoset—generally no more than four inches long—can be held in the palm of the hand. Marmosets are classified separately from New World monkeys because their fingers are tipped with slim, modified claws instead of the blunt nails common to most monkeys; marmosets have nails only on the big toe of each foot. Their thumbs are not opposable, so they cannot use their hands to grasp objects as efficiently as monkeys or even prosimians can.

For sheer appeal, however, marmosets outshine most of their primate relatives. Some, like the flamboyant golden marmoset, are maned like a lion. The coloration of marmosets is often distinctive, and the heads of some of these little animals are capped with eye-catching arrangements of sleek, glossy fur—European courtesans in the 17th century carried imported marmosets as fashion accessories.

The pygmy marmoset shown above may have bitten off more than it can chew. Even a small grasshopper is an ample mouthful for this simian.

Three tawny golden marmosets (right), totally absorbed in their task, pick insects out of the porous bark of a branch. Nearby, a youngster keeps an eye out for predators.

An alert pair of Geoffroy's marmosets, denizens of Panama's forests, rest in a treetop hideaway.

The sleek black Goeldi's marmoset below is a rare creature that is mysterious even to most zoologists. Little is known of its behavior in the wild.

Rats and Mice

Rodents are the largest order of mammals, both in number of species (more than 1,770) and in individuals (countless billions), outnumbering all other warm-blooded quadrupeds and bipeds combined. There is considerable variation in this order that includes beavers, porcupines, rats, lemmings, badgers and the familiar cage pets, gerbils and hamsters. Rodents are ubiquitous, inhabiting almost every continent, either as natives or as immigrants. Most are hypertense and forever on the alert for predators, since rodents are the principal item on the menus of most furred and feathered carnivores. The common denominator among rodents is their teeth—oversize, chisel-like incisors that grow constantly throughout their lives and that are kept sharp and trimmed by constant chewing on wood, nuts, plaster walls or other hard matter. Untrimmed, their teeth will grow into inward-curving tusks that can seriously injure or even kill them.

The most familiar rodents are rats and mice, whose usefulness as laboratory animals and as important links in the food chain is virtually unrivaled. In laboratories all over the world, domesticated rats and mice are the prime subjects of scientific experiments and research projects that aim to cure human diseases and determine the effects of myriad drugs on man. Because rodents are so similar to man in the adaptability of their eating habits, rats and mice are invaluable to scientists doing studies on diet and nutrition. Another asset is the rodents' life span; in the wild, rats and mice rarely live longer than one year because a large number of animals prey upon them, including snakes, dogs, cats, owls and hawks, but in captivity they may live as long as three years. Such a period is just right for studies on aging, growth and heredity. In addition, rats and mice are a perfect size to house and handle with ease in laboratories. In the United States alone scientific studies use some 18 million rats each year. It is the rare person who has not reaped, directly or indirectly, the benefits of the medical and psychological research done with these adaptable rodents.

But to most people, the destructiveness and havoc rats and mice wreak on the environment far outweigh any of their virtues. Yet the vast majority of rats and mice are actually beneficial and essential to the overall balance of nature; they furnish food for other animals and prey on insects, whose numbers they keep in check. These rodents should never be confused with the true villains of the order, the brown or Norway rat, the black rat and the innocent-looking house mouse. As carriers of plague, typhus, and other epidemic diseases this trio has inflicted death and misery on the world since prehistoric times. The Black Death, the most catastrophic plague in history, killed approximately one quarter of the population of medieval Europe and was almost certainly spread by rats, which serve as hosts for plague-bearing fleas.

Every year, one fifth of the world's crops are consumed by rats. Their depredation of the rice in Asia alone amounts to 48 million tons a year—enough to feed one quarter of a billion people. All the centuries of effort by man and nature to exterminate rodents have had little or no success. Rats have survived devastating drought and floods. They have developed resistance to the deadliest poisons and have even survived atomic bomb tests at Eniwetok. The rodents' uncanny ability to adapt and their awesome proliferation—it is estimated that a single pair of rats can produce 15,000 descendants in a year—have helped them play their dominant role.

Rats and mice have settled in cities, farms, countrysides and wildernesses, where they have adapted to nearly every kind of climate and environment, consuming almost any kind of food. Although there are some physical differences, mice are actually smaller versions of rats. Mice are usually rounder and have softer fur and poorer eyesight than their larger, more sinewy relatives. There are hundreds of different kinds of mice. The most common, the house mouse, has always lived close to man, in his houses and barns where it is warm and where food is easy to pilfer. In fair weather house mice may venture outside, where they, like rats, are considered garden pests. And they are carriers of the same dread diseases as their larger counterparts. There are some attractive species though, such as the dainty little white-footed deer mouse of North American forest lands and the long-tailed dormouse, immortalized in *Alice in Wonderland*. Some rats, too, have their winning ways. The giant rat of sub-Saharan Africa is the largest member of the family, having a length of 18 inches and a weight of two pounds. It is an amiable vegetarian that is popular in Africa both as a docile pet and as highly regarded food. Unfortunately, however, the reputation of the more attractive members of the order Rodentia and the beneficial role they play in nature only slightly offset the bad name acquired over the centuries by the whole tribe of rats and mice.

Bushy-tailed wood rat

A brown rat (left) gobbles the kernels from a dried ear of corn. Brown rats are distinguished by their relatively small ears and somewhat abbreviated tails, which are always shorter than their bodies. The brown rat is the black rat's worst enemy.

The Main Menaces

When it comes to the brown rat and the black rat, even the most ardent animal lovers reserve judgment. Among the 120 species in the genus *Rattus*—some of them are seen on the following pages—these two species pose the most serious threat to mankind as disease carriers and destroyers of crops, stock and property.

Natives of Asia, the brown and black rats arrived in Europe over land or by ship and then migrated to the Western Hemisphere on explorer and merchant vessels. Black rats, the superior seagoers, came first, soon joined and preyed upon by the larger, fiercer brown rats. Today the black rat is usually found in coastal areas; the brown rat has a virtually unrestricted range.

Both species tend to congregrate in large groups. Both are nest builders, but the black rat, a skillful climber, usually constructs its nest in trees or in the upper levels of buildings, while the burrowing brown rat sets up house under floors, in walls or in the ground. For both, the nest serves as a nursery for the young, which are born blind and deaf. They are cared for by their mothers in the nest until they are about three weeks old, when they are ready to join the rat community as adults.

Dried grasses and other vegetation make a meal for this sleek black rat (below). Like all rats, the black rat will eat almost anything that comes its way. Though usually solitary feeders, rats have been known to work together to overpower large targets such as pigs and chickens.

Cheek pouches stuffed to capacity, a kangaroo rat (right) pauses before scurrying back to its sandy burrow. Kangaroo rats are members of the pocket mouse family and inhabit arid areas in the western United States. They can go for extended periods —some for their entire lives— without water, obtaining necessary moisture from their food.

A nattily striped maned rat (above), looking more like a mini-porcupine than a rat, inches along a fallen log. A denizen of eastern Africa, this rat is named for the long, coarse, erectile hairs that extend from the nape of its neck, along its back partway down its tail, the end of which is tipped in pure white.

With its scant stubble of hair and its barely visible eyes and ears, the suitably named naked mole rat (right) looks more like a developing fetus than the mature adult it actually is. Naked mole rats are found in colonies under the sandy soil of parts of eastern Africa, where they live most of their lives in the maze of tunnels they dig.

An African giant pouched rat (below) plods through a pile of fallen cocoa pods. These large, 18-inch rodents are found throughout the continent's forested areas. They are timid and solitary creatures that usually maintain a nocturnal life-style although they sometimes forage during the day, when they behave as if they were blind, sitting upright and sniffing the air furiously.

How to Succeed

Wherever they are found, from Colombia, South America, north to Alaska and Labrador, deer mice are a successful species. Generally no more than eight inches in length, including their two- to four-inch tails, these adaptable animals have invaded almost every kind of habitat from forests and prairies to woodlands and tundras, and are often the most numerous mammals in the area. Not surprisingly, the deer mouse's diet rivals its habitat in diversity. It feeds on seeds, nuts, fruits and leaves, as well as on insects, spiders, worms and even carrion.

Deer mice like to travel under cover of darkness, and many will not even venture out on a moonlit night, taking shelter instead in nests they construct out of dried vegetation. These may be located in tunnels that the mice dig themselves, in abandoned burrows and birds' nests, in logs and trees. Deer mice groom themselves frequently and have equally high standards for their nests, which are left for new ones when the old ones become soiled.

A young deer mouse (left), eager to suckle, pursues its mother out onto a limb. A female deer mouse produces three to four litters every year, each averaging four young. Born naked, blind and toothless, the young are independent by the time they are six weeks old.

An abandoned bird's nest (left) serves as the foundation for a deer mouse's home. The mouse weaves a cupola of leaves, stems and twigs on top of the original structure and lines the interior with green vegetation. The entrance is closed when the mouse is inside.

A deer mouse (right) nibbles on leaves beside its arboreal nest. Preyed upon by almost every meat-eating animal, deer mice are of necessity shy and wary. Among themselves they seem to be quite communicative, producing squeaking and buzzing sounds. When alarmed, they pound the ground furiously with their front feet.

Mouse Medley

The standard mouse image is keyed to the common house mouse or perhaps the field mouse: a small, furry animal with a long tail, pointed snout, large black eyes and rounded ears. But the gallery of photographs on these pages illustrates that even within the limits of the popular image, there is great variety among the hundreds of species of mice. Some, like the jumping mouse, have naked, scaly tails; others, like the African dormouse, have a furry, brushlike appendage. Although they are all conservatively colored, they are of many shades within the gray-brown spectrum, and some animals, such as the striped grass mouse, sport coats with handsome patterns and designs.

White-footed mice

Striped grass mouse

Spiny mice

Jumping mice

House mouse

African dormouse

Harvest mice

The Mouse by H. H. Munro

The embarrassment of having a mouse running around inside one's clothes is rare in the experience of most well-bred gentlemen. But that is precisely the predicament, arising aboard a train, that confronts the hero of The Mouse, *a short story by H. H. Munro, who wrote under the pen name Saki.*

Without being actually afraid of mice, Theodoric classed them among the coarser incidents of life, and considered that Providence, with a little exercise of moral courage, might long ago have recognized that they were not indispensable, and have withdrawn them from circulation. As the train glided out of the station Theodoric's nervous imagination accused himself of exhaling a weak odour of stableyard, and possibly of displaying a mouldy straw or two on his usually well-brushed garments. Fortunately the only other occupant of the compartment, a lady of about the same age as himself, seemed inclined for slumber rather than scrutiny; the train was not due to stop till the terminus was reached, in about an hour's time, and the carriage was of the old-fashioned sort, that held no communication with a corridor, therefore no further travelling companions were likely to intrude on Theodoric's semi-privacy. And yet the train had scarcely attained its normal speed before he became reluctantly but vividly aware that he was not alone with the slumbering lady; he was not even alone in his own clothes. A warm, creeping movement over his flesh betrayed the unwelcome and highly resented presence, unseen but poignant, of a strayed mouse, that had evidently dashed into its present retreat during the episode of the pony harnessing. Furtive stamps and shakes and wildly directed pinches failed to dislodge the intruder, whose motto, indeed, seemed to be Excelsior; and the lawful occupant of the clothes lay back against the cushions and endeavoured rapidly to evolve some means for putting an end to the dual ownership. It was unthinkable that he should continue for the space of a whole hour in the horrible position of a Rowton House for vagrant mice (already his imagination had at least doubled the numbers of the alien invasion). On the other hand, nothing less drastic than partial disrobing would ease him of his tormentor, and to undress in the presence of a lady, even for so laudable a purpose, was an idea that made his eartips tingle in a blush of abject shame. He had never been able to bring himself even to the mild exposure of open-work socks in the presence of the fair sex. And yet—the lady in this case was to all appearances soundly and securely asleep; the mouse, on the other hand, seemed to be trying to crowd a Wanderjahr into a few strenuous minutes. If there is any truth in the theory of transmigration, this particular mouse must certainly have been in a former state a member of the Alpine Club. Sometimes in its eagerness it lost its footing and slipped for half an inch or so; and then, in fright, or more probably temper, it bit. Theodoric was goaded into the most audacious undertaking of his life. Crimsoning to the hue of a beetroot and keeping an agonized watch on his slumbering fellow-traveller, he swiftly and noiselessly secured the ends of his railway-rug to the racks on either side of the carriage, so that a substantial curtain hung athwart the compartment. In the narrow dressing-room that he had thus improvised he proceeded with violent haste to extricate himself partially and the mouse entirely from the surrounding casings of

tweed and half-wool. As the unravelled mouse gave a wild leap to the floor, the rug, slipping its fastening at either end, also came down with a heart-curdling flop, and almost simultaneously the awakened sleeper opened her eyes. With a movement almost quicker than the mouse's, Theodoric pounced on the rug, and hauled its ample folds chin-high over his dismantled person as he collapsed into the further corner of the carriage. The blood raced and beat in the veins of his neck and forehead, while he waited dumbly for the communication-cord to be pulled. The lady, however, contented herself with a silent stare at her strangely muffled companion. How much had she seen, Theodoric queried to himself, and in any case what on earth must she think of his present posture?

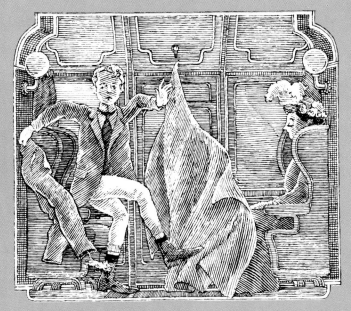

"I think I have caught a chill," he ventured desperately.

"Really, I'm sorry," she replied. "I was just going to ask you if you would open this window."

"I fancy it's malaria," he added, his teeth chattering slightly, as much from fright as from a desire to support his theory.

"I've got some brandy in my hold-all, if you'll kindly reach it down for me," said his companion.

"Not for worlds—I mean, I never take anything for it," he assured her earnestly.

"I suppose you caught it in the Tropics?"

Theodoric, whose acquaintance with the Tropics was limited to an annual present of a chest of tea from an uncle in Ceylon, felt that even the malaria was slipping from him. Would it be possible, he wondered, to disclose the real state of affairs to her in small instalments?

"Are you afraid of mice?" he ventured, growing, if possible, more scarlet in the face.

"Not unless they came in quantities, like those that ate up Bishop Hatto. Why do you ask?"

"I had one crawling inside my clothes just now," said Theodoric in a voice that hardly seemed his own. "It was a most awkward situation."

"It must have been, if you wear your clothes at all tight," she observed; "but mice have strange ideas of comfort."

"I had to get rid of it while you were asleep," he continued; then, with a gulp, he added, "it was getting rid of it that brought me to—to this."

"Surely leaving off one small mouse wouldn't bring on a chill," she exclaimed, with a levity that Theodoric accounted abominable.

Evidently she had detected something of his predicament, and was enjoying his confusion. All the blood in his body seemed to have mobilized in one concentrated blush, and an agony of abasement, worse than a myriad mice, crept up and down over his soul. And then, as reflection began to assert itself, sheer terror took the place of humiliation. With every minute that passed the train was rushing nearer to the crowded and bustling terminus where dozens of prying eyes would be exchanged for the one paralyzing pair that watched him from the further corner of the carriage. There was one slender despairing chance, which the next few minutes must decide. His fellow-traveller might relapse into a blessed slumber. But as the minutes throbbed by that chance ebbed away. The furtive glance which Theodoric stole at her from time to time disclosed only an unwinking wakefulness.

"I think we must be getting near now," she presently observed.

Theodoric had already noted with growing terror the recurring stacks of small, ugly dwellings that heralded the journey's end. The words acted as a signal. Like a hunted beast breaking cover and dashing madly towards some other haven of momentary safety he threw aside his rug, and struggled frantically into his dishevelled garments. He was conscious of dull suburban stations racing past the window, of a choking, hammering sensation in his throat and heart, and of an icy silence in that corner towards which he dared not look. Then as he sank back in his seat, clothed and almost delirious, the train slowed down to a final crawl, and the woman spoke.

"Would you be so kind," she asked, "as to get me a porter to put me into a cab? It's a shame to trouble you when you're feeling unwell, but being blind makes one so helpless at a railway station."

Nemeses

Thanks to a variety of predators, the ever-burgeoning rodent population remains tenuously under control, and rats and mice seldom live more than one or two years. Their predators, owls, hawks, snakes and weasels, play a vital role in maintaining a balanced ecosystem, making excellent use of specialized hunting techniques to capture their victims. In dealing with the alert rodents, which have a keen sense of hearing, the silent approach proves best. The long-eared owl, for example, has a fringe of flight feathers on the edge of each wing that let it ride wind currents and muffle its sound as the bird zeroes in on its target. The corn snake also takes a stealthy approach, and before the rodent

has a chance to resist, the snake coils its body around its helpless victim and suffocates it.

The role of these predators is crucial since rats and mice constitute about one third of the world's mammals. There are more brown rats than people in North America today —a fact that demonstrates both their adaptability and their reproductive rate. Under favorable climatic conditions, breeding continues the year round. Rats and mice have from three to six litters a year, averaging six offspring per litter. Thus, theoretically, a single pair of these prolific rodents could be the progenitors of as many as 15,000 descendants within their lifetime.

The jaws of a corn snake (above) close relentlessly over the body of a rat. These beautifully patterned reptiles frequent the cornfields where rodents flourish.

If the talons of the long-eared owl (opposite) do not deal a rat its death blow, its beak will. Rodents, which are swallowed whole, make up 80 percent of the owl's diet.

Big-Time Breeders

Like their cousins the rats and mice, voles and lemmings are two of the most prolific species of mammals. Females become sexually mature when they are only 25 days old. Voles breed all year round, and lemmings reproduce throughout the spring, summer and fall, adding several litters a year to the communities in which they live. Each litter may consist of as many as nine pink, hairless young. In their endless fecundity, females can become pregnant while they are still nursing an earlier litter.

Lemming and vole populations vary greatly in size from year to year—fluctuations that seem to run in three- to four-year cycles, perhaps based on availability of food. One vole colony increased twentyfold during a single four-year period. Such drastic increases create serious overcrowding and scarcity of food within the communities and force many members to leave. The seemingly obsessive hunt by the lemmings of Scandinavia for new food sources is legendary. While in reality the vast majority die of starvation and disease during their trek across the landscape, the myth has a suicidal ending: A handful of others continue on until they reach the sea. They plunge in and swim until, overcome by exhaustion, they drown.

Two russet-backed bank voles (right) crouch next to a fallen log. Bank voles like to nest in the crevices of logs, rock ledges and trees, and will often use a hollow stump as a storage bin, packing it with up to two gallons of food.

A mother water vole (left) stands guard over her babies, who growl and chatter from their nest of shredded leaves. Voles are attentive mothers, always moving their young from a disturbed nest, and keeping both babies and nest immaculate.

Blending well with its rocky background, a lemming (right) stands up to investigate its surroundings before continuing on its perpetual search for food. The lemming turns white in winter, the only rodent to do so.

The Great Migrations

by Georges Blond

In his extensive study of animal migration, The Great Migrations, *Georges Blond—acknowledging man's inability to explain the legendary journeys of the lemming—gives the floor, in a literary fantasy, to an expert: an observant lemming who, in the excerpt below, chronicles the events leading up to a mass exodus.*

I kept my taste for these solitary walks even after I had founded a family. My mate took care of the young, occasionally making excursions of her own. Once the young were grown, I left her and returned to my own little nest. Such was our monotonously peaceful, happy life, the life of millions of little people who never cause talk.

One day toward the end of winter, I left my nest in the burrow for one of the exits from our underground city. Certain galleries opened up near bushes or trees whose bark was particularly tasty, and I had a sudden longing for fresh food. Along the way I was overtaken by three lemmings who, instead of following me quietly, pushed ahead. One of them even emitted an irritated cry. These manners surprised me. When I reached the exit, I looked prudently around to see what was going on outside.

The snowy ground glistened in the light of the moon, punctuated by dark masses of rock. A few steps away some lemmings were nibbling at the bark of dwarf birches. I hadn't expected to see so many. Crawling clumps of them swarmed over the snow-covered bushes, transforming them into little islands of black amid the general whiteness. They did not eat in the usual restrained way, but wriggled and pushed one another around, as they streamed first toward the trees and then away, bumping and crying aloud. Farther off, other lemmings were leaping in the snow, and beyond them in every direction were others still. What utter madness! I shouldn't have been surprised to hear that some rash creatures, overcome by cold and fatigue, were lying frozen and dead. What a killing a silent, predatory owl could have made, had it swooped down upon this unruly conglomeration!

Two other lemmings came, or rather burst, out of the burrow beside me. They shot forward, whirled around a group nibbling at one of the bushes, and then ran on until they were gone from sight. While I was staring at this most unusual spectacle, my heart began to beat faster. I stood hesitantly at the exit, waiting for the most favorable moment to proceed, when gradually an urge to run and leap with my fellows came over me. I had lost and forgotten the hunger for fresh food which had brought me this far. At present, I wanted to move, in a way I had never imagined before, and my heart was beating faster and faster. I threw myself forward, leaping and running in circles through the snow. I rushed into a crowd of my fellows, shoving them aside, in order to have a taste of the birch bark. But a few bites were quite enough. I turned around and pressed back through the mob. I didn't even know that, like the others, I was emitting shrill cries.

How long this excitement lasted, I have not the remotest idea. At a certain point I had a sensation of piercing cold in my nose. Apparently I hadn't altogether lost my reason, because I immediately obeyed this warning signal and plunged back into the burrow. The gallery was crowded with lemmings who, like myself, were trying to reach their nests while others pressed toward the outside. We knocked against one another in the darkness, still crying. At last I got to my nest and, dead-tired, fell into a deep sleep.

The series of events I have just described took place several times in succession. Every time it began in the same way: I woke up to hear a loud, shuffling noise in the galleries, and immediately I too felt an urge to dash about outside. When I came back I was invariably exhausted; but day by day the period of sleeping grew shorter, and I would wake abruptly, to hear shuffling and cries. Our underground city, which once upon a time had been such an oasis of peace, was now a place of tumult and disorder, to which I was increasingly unwilling to return. And I was aware that the other lemmings felt the same way. We were no longer happy, but none of us could tell why.

Winter was over. At first the sun only grazed the snow but then it rose gradually higher above the horizon. We lemmings went out, still tumultuously, into the long twilight and ate greedily of the vegetation bared by the

melting snow. We ventured far from the burrow, and many of us fell victim to the silent swoop of an owl or to a buzzard dropping like a stone out of the sky. Almost every day an ermine came out of the rocks. Before we had any inkling of its presence it was among us, a flash of white zigzagging over the ground; and as we fled in terror we heard the victims' cries. But nothing seemed to teach us a lesson. The next day we ventured forth just as rashly as before, and were just as reluctant to go home.

About this time I began to understand why we were less and less contented with our underground city: the place was overpopulated. We still had our individual and family nests; but they were too close together, and the galleries were always crowded. We dug into the earth in order to widen them, and this caused parts of the roof and walls to crumble. We seemed to be destroying our own burrow, and it became all the more detestable, so that now we ac-

tively wanted to go away. But where? When we went outside there were so many of us that we felt uncomfortable and ill at ease. I wanted to escape, not only from the noisy, overcrowded burrow, but also from the mass of lemmings all over our domain, to recover somehow the peace and quiet I had known in other days. This very nostalgia served to disquiet me, and I could see that the same was true of my fellows. All of us were in constant irritation, and every meeting served as the pretext for a quarrel. Instead of rubbing noses in friendly fashion, we uttered shrill cries, spat in one another's faces and fought ferociously.

As the days lengthened, the mating season came around. But that which had been so pleasurable in other years was now sheer hell. Desire was overpowering, and our new pugnaciousness caused us to fight over possession of the females, in spite of the fact that there were plenty of them. At the least affront lemmings fought to the death.

We do not eat flesh of any kind, and the dead bodies rotted and raised a stench on the ground.

Into this horrid atmosphere the new generation was born. Amazingly enough, the little ones grew faster than their parents and grandparents; they soon became just as active, excitable, and hostile as ourselves. We realized into what fantastic disorder our race had fallen when we saw young males, at an age when we had been hardly more than children, seeking out the females and fighting furiously for them. And the worst of it was that we ourselves suddenly had the same desire and found ourselves battling with our own progeny just as we had recently battled among ourselves. Females who up to that time had produced one or two litters a year now brought forth three or even four, and their daughters gave birth beside them.

It was obvious that this state of things could not endure. Our city was uninhabitable; we had all reached a climax of exasperation and felt an overpowering urge to go, to go anywhere at all as long as it was far enough away. Our departure took place one morning, when swarming crowds of lemmings were clustered about every exit from the burrow. At a certain moment this promiscuity was so unpleasant that I clambered up onto the branch of a tree, whence I had a view of all our people. The sight was distressing and comic at the same time. Lemmings ran and leaped in every direction, crying aloud and biting one another. Suddenly a single male emerged from the crowd immediately below me. He ran in the direction opposite to that of the sun and started down over the edge of the cliff. None of us had ever left the plateau. But this fellow dared to cross our natural boundary and to keep right on going, apparently with no intention of turning back.

His example produced an instantaneous and dynamic effect. Four, ten, thirty lemmings ran after him, over the cliff and then straight ahead, as if some madness were propelling them. I looked hard, and my heart pounded. A second later, I jumped down from the tree and followed. When I reached the edge of the plateau I turned around and saw a great column of lemmings speeding toward me. Some remained near the openings of the burrow, and a few had even gone back inside; but the immense majority was scurrying toward me. We all went over the cliff, in a solid brown torrent, together.

Squirrels and Marmots

One of the most familiar rodent families is the Sciuridae, the squirrels. The word *squirrel* conjures up a picture of a frisky, plume-tailed tree dweller, a cheeky creature of city parks and woodlands competing with pigeons and starlings for the handouts of humans. But this description really fits only one variety—the tree squirrel. The Sciuridae also include the ground squirrels, most of which bear very little resemblance to their tree-dwelling brethren.

Tree squirrels are characterized by an oversize tail, often nearly as long as the animal itself, which serves as a balancing pole in arboreal acrobatics, a parasol in sunny weather and a blanket in winter. The prototypal eastern gray squirrel, with its air of cocky assurance, is a study in perpetual motion. It is usually extremely wary, chattering constantly while keeping an eye on interlopers from behind a tree trunk. But in areas where it lives close to man, the eastern gray (the western version is distinguished by its white underbelly) becomes quite trusting, accepting nuts from the hands of humans and even moving into attics and barns. Closely related to the gray, but bearing no resemblance to a fox, the larger eastern fox squirrel is a denizen of open woodlands. It is a less than agile climber and builds its nest of leaves in the hollow of a tree. The eastern fox squirrel is a late sleeper that begins foraging rather late in the morning and does not stop until after the sun has set.

North American tree squirrels are primarily diurnal animals. Only the flying squirrels, diminutive—12 inches or less—creatures of timberlands in the United States and Canada, never venture out before dark. The flying squirrel is easily identified by the folding flaps of skin extending along each side of its body from its front to its rear leg. These enable it to glide from tree to tree for distances of as much as 50 to 60 feet in its nightly search for nuts, berries and other tidbits. The African tropics are home to numerous species of tree squirrels, all of which resemble their North American relatives in general appearance. The giant forest squirrel, however, is distinguished by its very bushy foot-long tail, which is ringed in black and white, while the four-striped squirrel has, as its name implies, four bold, black stripes running down the length of its brown-colored or olive-green-colored back. The Gambian sun squirrel is the only savanna-dwelling tree squirrel. Due to the variable climate of its habitat, this squirrel is thought to store food to use during the dry season.

As thrifty provisioners, tree squirrels are well known for laying away winter supplies of nuts and acorns to get them through the cold months. In doing so they make a strange contribution to their environment: While they usually have a cache near their winter quarters from which they draw provender in cold weather, they also bury nuts in other spots as far as 100 yards from home. Since these deposits are frequently forgotten or abandoned by the rodents, the plantings amount to a small-scale reforestation project, leading one to think of squirrels as the Johnny Appleseeds of the animal kingdom.

The groundling members of the squirrel family are a mixed lot that includes stocky creatures like the woodchuck as well as the nimble chipmunk. Woodchucks (or groundhogs), creatures of flatlands and prairies, keep their underground dens fastidiously neat and use sanitary dumps, or latrines, outside the entrances. Marmots have adapted to a mountainous habitat in the North American West, Europe and Asia. The hoary marmot, a native of Alaska, is the largest member of the squirrel family, reaching a maximum length of 27 inches, including nine inches of well-furred tail.

The smallest of the ground squirrels are the chipmunks, the graceful, beautifully striped creatures that are often seen frisking around stone walls or at the entrances to their dens, standing on their haunches to nibble a nut or to watch for danger. Like all diggers, chipmunks hibernate in winter. But like the tree squirrels, which do not hibernate, chipmunks keep a handy supply of food in their burrows in case they awaken from their torpor while the weather above ground is still freezing.

Pocket gophers, members of a closely related family, excavate more elaborate burrows than the ground squirrels. The main tunnel of the pocket gopher's burrow may stretch 500 feet or more. Pocket gophers are familiar animals over most of North America west of the Mississippi. They have large, sturdy front claws for digging and a nearly naked tail that acts like an organ of touch, as a human finger does, and can be used to guide the gopher when it retreats backward—as it sometimes does—through its warren. Its distinguishing feature, however, is a pair of external, reversible cheek pouches that can be filled through slits on either side of its mouth. The pocket gropher crams these repositories with food for leisurely consumption in the safety of its burrow.

Ground squirrels

A European red eats away at a mushroom (left). Instead of consuming these delicacies on the spot, the squirrel may harvest and store them for future use.

A solicitous parent (opposite) unceremoniously transports a wandering red squirrel youngster that has strayed too far from the safety of its den.

Two handsome, bright-eyed squirrels enjoy a quiet picnic (below). Their powerful teeth can pry open a pine cone in record time, exposing the edible seeds.

Alert Europeans

The range of the European red tree squirrel spans the Eurasian continent and extends beyond, to the British Isles in the west and Japan in the east. The animal often settles in coniferous or mixed woodlands, where the seeds of cone-bearing trees, the principal item of its diet, are plentiful. Although it must spend a good deal of time scurrying about on the forest floor, gathering up a variety of edibles, the red squirrel usually eats its meal in its nest in some high, sheltered tree niche.

This nest—a globular mass of sticks and twigs—is tucked into the fork of a tree or arranged on a sturdy branch. As an alternative, a squirrel sometimes appropriates an abandoned woodpecker hole or hollow tree trunk, insulating the ready-made den with layers of bark and leaves to protect it from the elements. Squirrels often have a few less elaborate temporary nests throughout their territory. They may retreat to these satellite homes to shelter from the heat or to enjoy a brief respite from periods of frenetic activity.

During the warmer months the energetic rodents scamper about, providently storing up food and burying it in shallow underground caches. These reserves—none very large—will be drawn upon during the winter months. Tree squirrels depend on a keen sense of smell to relocate the hidden stores, and in some of the more inhospitable environments inclement weather may complicate their retrieval. But even a thick layer of snow does not prevent a squirrel from finding the scent.

83

Treetop Nursery

The red squirrels of North America are tree squirrels, as adept as their European cousins are at scrambling about through the canopy of greenery high above the forest floor. Although they are primarily arboreal, they regularly descend to the ground to forage for food. Occasionally they dig burrows in the loose soil under rotten logs or boulders, excavating multichambered tunnels in which they nest or store excess food. More frequently, however, the permanent nest is an arboreal one. If a cozy tree hollow is not available, the squirrel will construct its own nest, built about five feet from the treetop and as high as 65 feet above ground. Made of twigs, bark and leaves, the nest is where the squirrel feeds, rests, shelters from inclement weather, gives birth and nurtures its offspring.

Young are born in late spring and early summer, although females may produce a second litter in late summer. The babies are hairless, blind, pink and helpless. It takes about 27 days for their eyes to open and at least that long for the fur to grow in. At about this time the young begin venturing out of the den, and shortly thereafter they are weaned. Although they remain close to their mother through the summer, by early fall—inquisitive, independent and very active—they are ready to brave the challenges of forest life.

A young red squirrel (opposite) hesitates before leaving its comfortable, sequestered den. Until its eyes open it will remain vulnerable—unequipped even to make the first tentative move toward independence.

Their eyes just beginning to open, three young red squirrels (right) cling to each other as they begin to develop a feel for arboreal life. In a few weeks they will start to move out of the nest, but until then their mother will keep a close watch on the brood.

Hill Country Harvest by Hal Borland

Born in Nebraska, raised in Colorado, Hal Borland developed a love of nature early in his life. Though he moved east to pursue a journalistic career, his ardor for wild things did not diminish. The excerpt below, taken from Borland's Hill Country Harvest, *tells of the "spring planting" activities of a gray squirrel on the author's front lawn.*

There are, I suppose, two ways of looking at it. So I shall be charitable. This squirrel was being helpful rather than critical. The lawn here at the side and the back is a little mangy in spots and I haven't had time to reseed as I suppose I should. This fellow—he is a male; the females are busy taking care of the small children just now—had been looking over the place for some time, and he knew what had to be done, so he did it. And I should thank him, even if the lawn turns out to be a corn patch.

It happened just the other morning. I glanced out the window and saw this gray squirrel on the side lawn with an ear of corn in his mouth. He had come from the corn crib, where he has a private entrance, and I expected him to climb the big Norway spruce, as usual, and sit on a favorite branch and eat his fill of corn germ, spitting out the bulk of the kernels. But he didn't. He laid the ear on the ground, carefully chose one kernel from the middle of the ear, held it in his teeth, found a bare spot in the lawn, and dug a hole with his forepaws. He tucked the kernel in the hole, patted it carefully with his nose, then covered it with a dozen deft strokes of his paws. Just as neatly as Barbara planting squash seeds.

He went back to the ear, chose another kernel, found another bare spot in the lawn and made another planting.

He planted six kernels within a 3-foot circle, then picked up the seed ear, moved a little way, and did the same thing again. He worked the whole side yard, planting, by actual count, thirty-two kernels of corn. By then he had cleaned off the center of the ear, making it look like a dumbbell. I watched carefully and didn't see him eat even one kernel. He discarded several kernels, probably sterile seed, though how he knew I can't even guess. If I were a skeptical scientist I should plant those discarded seeds in a flower pot and see if they germinate. But I'm not that much of a skeptic. I know they won't.

Finished with the side yard, he moved back alongside the woodshed, where the lawn is particularly ratty. There he planted thirty-nine kernels. This I noticed, though: At the back of the yard is a barbed wire fence separating lawn from pasture, and Mr. Squirrel didn't plant one kernel of corn beyond the fence, in the pasture. Don't ask me why. I'm just a human being with limited understanding. But I know that if corn is planted in the pasture the cows will eat

it. Maybe the squirrel knows that too. He should. He has watched the cows.

Finished alongside the woodshed, he took his seed ear around the shed and resumed his work back of the house. A crow came and perched in an apple tree nearby, watching. The squirrel glanced at the crow, then went on about his business. And the crow didn't come down to get either the ear of corn or the kernels the squirrel was hiding. I rather wished the crow would make a try, to see what happened.

I lost count while the squirrel was working in the back yard, but he finally had that ear of corn stripped down to half a dozen rows at each end. Then he decided he had done enough for me. He picked up the ear, had a good look around, and went loping across the pasture to a big elm a hundred yards away. I watched him with the field glasses while he climbed to a comfortable crotch and tucked the ear with its remaining kernels into a favorite pantry corner. He ate none of it. He tucked it away, came down, and went off into the woods.

No challenge, it seems, is too great for some gray squirrels—whether it is swimming down a cold woodland stream (top), or executing a tricky downward swoop to reach a cluster of tempting oak buds (above). The enterprising scavenger at right has taken pains to haul its booty up into a live oak tree to enjoy it in safety.

88

The Versatile Grays

While red squirrels generally establish themselves in coniferous forests, eastern gray tree squirrels usually prefer the hardwood tree zones from Ontario and New Brunswick south to Florida. They feed on the seeds and nuts of beechnut, hickory and oak trees, prying them open skillfully and quickly with their lower incisors. Gray squirrels are not exclusively vegetarian, however, and an inattentive mother bird may lose one or two nestlings or a clutch of her eggs to a hungry squirrel.

Grays are more gregarious and sociable than red squirrels and less aggressive. They do not generally object to the presence of other grays in their territory unless they are in competition for a diminishing or scarce food supply. In that case, a gray will confront an interloper squarely and attempt to frighten it away. This is ordinarily a show of false bravado, but on the rare occasions when a conflict ensues, it can be fierce. A female will put up an especially vigorous fight if she is defending her nesting young.

A startled-looking flying squirrel (left) peeks out of its den. Constantly on the alert for threats to its survival, it watches out for great horned owls swooping down from above and tree snakes that can creep up stealthily from below.

A flying squirrel soars through the air at a dizzying height (opposite). Using its tail as a rudder, it positions its body carefully to land squarely on its well-padded feet. By angling its tail upward, the squirrel can brake its glide, enabling it to alight on the vertical surface of a tree trunk.

Mimicking Flight

Flying squirrels cannot actually fly. Their name is inspired by their looping tree-to-tree leaps, which, aided by membranous flaps resembling wings on either side of their bodies, have a rhythm and fluidity that mimic the movements of flight. Preparing to launch itself, the squirrel lowers its head and gives itself a push with its legs to gain momentum. Starting from a height of 50 feet or more, a flying squirrel coasts downward, and the descending arc of the glide path may extend as much as 150 feet if the squirrel is proficient and the air currents favorable. By manipulating its flaps, the animal regulates the speed and direction of descent, negotiating sharp right-angle turns effortlessly. Flying squirrels remain in their arboreal dens until nightfall and then swarm out to feed. If alarmed during the day, they may—though very rarely—venture out to reconnoiter the situation.

Striped Storers

Chipmunks are one of the most familiar of all the ground squirrels. They are distinguished from their striped cousins by the distinctive pattern on their backs—five dark stripes alternating with four light ones. The coats of these small animals tend to echo the tones of their environment, and since they can be found in North America as well as Asia, the coloring of different species varies greatly—but the five-to-four stripe design is omnipresent.

During the winter, chipmunks, unlike other ground squirrels, do not go into true hibernation, the trancelike state in which animals are inactive until spring. Instead, they enter a dormant state during severe weather from which they awaken when it warms up even temporarily, when they snack on stored food. Thus while other ground squirrels are gorging themselves in summer and fall to put on the layer of fat that takes them through the sleeping season, the chipmunk is busy gathering food to nibble on during its waking time. After filling its cheek pouches, the chipmunk returns to its burrow, spits out the food and hurries off for more. Chipmunks will sometimes retire into their burrows during the hottest part of the summer—a form of behavior called estivation.

A cautious eastern chipmunk (opposite) stands next to a clump of hawkweed and looks around for danger. Chipmunks have very good eyesight. If a chipmunk hears a noise, it will try to spot the source and identify it visually before retreating.

A least chipmunk (below) stuffs its internal cheek pouches with goldenrod. Chipmunks will eat fruit, seeds, some insects and even birds' eggs. They usually select a stump, rock or other elevated lookout for a feeding station and will carry a meal there in their pouches.

The Chipmunk's Day

by Randall Jarrell

In his poem "A Chipmunk's Day," *Randall Jarrell, the American critic and poet, captures the self-sufficiency and peaceful demeanor of one of nature's most appealing creatures.*

In and out the bushes, up the ivy,
Into the hole
By the oak stump, the chipmunk flashes.
Up the pole

To the feeder full of seeds he dashes,
Stuffs his cheeks,
The chickadee and titmouse scold him.
Down he streaks.

Red as the leaves the wind blows off the maple,
Red as a fox,
Striped like a skunk, the chipmunk whistles
Past the love seat, past the mailbox,

Down the path,
Home to his warm hole stuffed with sweet
Things to eat.
Neat and slight and shining, his front feet

Curled at his breast, he sits there while the sun
Stripes the red west
With its last light: the chipmunk
Dives to his rest.

An Olympic marmot stands upright on the large, high mound that it
has constructed around the entrance to its den. These mounds, often
measuring four or five feet in diameter, are used by marmots as sun
decks and watchtowers.

Outsize Squirrel

As an excuse for a tongue twister (if a woodchuck could chuck wood) and as a legendary February forecaster of spring's arrival, the woodchuck (or groundhog) is well known. Woodchuck is the name generally given to those species in the genus *Marmota* found in the eastern United States. The natives of the western states are called marmots. The largest members of the squirrel family, marmots are primarily terrestrial animals that can climb and swim fairly well, and can run up to 10 mph to escape danger.

Outside rhyme and folklore, woodchucks are notorious as garden pests in the eastern United States. In the west, their cousins, such as the Olympic and hoary marmots, are also called rock chucks, or whistlers, for the warning sound they make. These marmots live quietly under ledges, within rocky crevices or in alpine meadows. Both forms hibernate through the cold months. During hibernation, a marmot's torpor is so deep that it can be dug out of its hole and handled for hours without being awakened.

In the sequence at right, two hoary marmots circle each other threateningly (top) and then close in to fight for possession of a burrow. Hoary marmots are the largest and loudest marmots. They can grow to 27 inches, weigh up to 15 pounds and emit a piercing alarm whistle.

South American Rodents

For at least 60 million years, South America drifted out of contact with the rest of the world, an isolated island continent much like Australia. Until the Central American land bridge rose out of the sea between two and three million years ago, linking the continent to North America, the animals of South America evolved as independent species, and many are like no other creatures on earth. After the appearance of the land bridge, animals from the north began to invade South America, and vice versa. Today the fauna is a rich and distinctive mix, living in a diversity of environments and climates—from desert to pampas to eternal snows on mountaintops to huge, dense tropical rain forests.

Like much other wildlife of South America, many of its rodents are unique. Of 16 rodent families that are native to the continent, 11 exist nowhere else. The most notable of these, and the largest of all rodents, is the capybara, which looks like a four-foot-long, 150-pound guinea pig. Capybaras live close to water either on the banks of rivers or in woods with dense vegetation, where they feed on shoreline and aquatic plants. They are excellent swimmers that take to water to escape their enemies—principally the jaguar—and they can swim underwater for considerable distances. But the water is not always a safe haven, for jaguars can pursue them there, and a number of aquatic creatures, such as alligators and anacondas, also savor the capybara's flesh. The big, piglike creatures are hunted by man as well, and are even raised commercially on ranches in Argentina.

Many of the rodents of South America are edible and have suffered from overhunting as a consequence. The vizcacha is a burrowing creature of the plains and mountains. The mountain species is systematically being exterminated for its food value, and the plains species is hunted as a pest and destroyer of sheep-grazing lands. Vizcachas live in communities of 20 to 30 in vast and complex underground warrens called vizcacheras, which they share amiably with foxes, snakes, lizards and owls. Male vizcachas are easily distinguished from females by their thick, prominent moustaches.

Chinchillas have been hounded to extinction or to near extinction in the wild for their fur, which is one of the softest and most valuable in the world. Although the mouselike chinchillas are now protected in their native habitat high in the Peruvian Andes, none have been seen there in many years and they have probably been extirpated. They survive, however, on commercial chinchilla ranches, where they are bred for their esteemed silvery fur. Another valuable rodent of South America is the coypu, which also is extensively bred for its luxuriant pelt in the United States and Europe, where it has been introduced, as well as in South America. The little creature is known in the fur trade as nutria. Coypus are adroit escape artists, and so many of them have managed to get away from commercial fur farms in the Northern Hemisphere that large numbers have become feral animals in the bayous of Louisiana and in Europe. These wild coypus are considered pests in many places because of the damage they do to crops and to irrigation ditches and dams.

Numerous other rodents of the southern regions of the New World have exotic-sounding names and strange idiosyncracies that mark them as very individual animals. The agouti was once a commonplace animal from Mexico to southernmost Brazil. In the wild, agoutis live in communal groups of as many as 40 animals, and they have such docile natures that they are easily tamed and are common household pets. The gopherlike tuco-tuco gets its name from the sound it makes: The unearthly noise from a burrowed colony, welling up from the entrances to the burrows, has been likened to the din of an underworld of gnomes hammering away inside their mines. Although the mara, or Patagonian cavy, looks like a long-eared, long-legged rabbit, it is a true rodent. It has an interesting mating rite: The male squirts a jet of urine at the female of his choice, a practice also common to the agoutis, certain porcupines, and rabbits and hares.

The quintessential South American rodent is the guinea pig, which is neither a pig nor a native of Guinea. Its name derives from the Guineamen, vessels that carried slaves to South America from Africa and then sailed to Europe with cargos that included the small rodents. When Pizarro and the Spanish conquistadores arrived in Peru, they found that the guinea pig had been kept for centuries as a domestic animal—a culinary tidbit—by the Incas. Nowadays guinea pigs are more often found in the domesticated state than in the wild. Clean, prolific, durable animals, they rank with rabbits and white rats as popular pets. They have also proven to be first-rate laboratory animals, so widely used in biomedical research that their name has become a synonym for all experimental subjects, including humans.

The Heavyweight

At a weight of over 150 pounds and with a length of up to four feet, the capybara is the largest rodent in the world. Found from eastern Panama southward to the region of South America lying east of the Andes, this stocky, stub-tailed creature with short legs and a blunt muzzle is one of the few mammals in South America whose survival is relatively secure. The capybara owes its success to its ability to adapt. An active, diurnal animal in those areas where it is undisturbed, the capybara has become wary and nocturnal where it is hunted by man for its fat and flesh.

Capybaras are sociable animals that live in bands or family groups of up to 20 members. They are completely herbivorous and spend much of the day nibbling shoots and grasses with their prominent incisors. Capybaras are semiaquatic in their habits and are rarely found far from water, which they use as a refuge when threatened or pursued. Propelled by partially webbed feet, they are superb swimmers and are able to stay completely submerged for considerable distances. Otherwise, they expose only their eyes, ears and noses as they swim. When they are undisturbed, capybaras come onto dry land, where they like to bask in the sun.

Mating between capybaras takes place all year long on land or in water, but intensifies during the spring rainy season. Females gestate for 15 to 16 weeks before giving birth to litters of two to eight young. Within hours after birth, capybaras are on their feet, following closely behind their mothers as they forage for vegetation.

Displaying its unmistakable snub-nosed profile (right), a male capybara pauses in a thicket of tall grasses. Male and female capybaras look almost identical. A distinguishing feature is the shiny black sebaceous gland that year-old males develop on their muzzles.

A sidelong glance is the only sign that this partially submerged capybara (below) even notices the jacana perched on its back. In the presence of a real enemy like a jaguar, puma, alligator or anaconda, a capybara would be far more alert.

Overleaf, a band of capybaras, including adults and their young, relax on the bank of a river. During the heat of the day entire bands often squeeze together into one mud wallow to escape the sun's rays.

Caribbean Treasure

by Ivan Sanderson

Raised in the bleak chill of Edinburgh, Scotland, Ivan Sanderson understandably chose to pursue his interest in animals in the warmth of the Caribbean and South American tropics. It was here that Sanderson came to know a most distinctive animal, the capybara. This passage from Caribbean Treasure *introduces the reader to this dignified creature—which, though bred in the wild, could also be at home in London's Hyde Park or the Bois de Boulogne in Paris.*

The capybara, on the other hand, is the most dignified, gentle, and lovable of all living creatures. We had one as a pet, and a more adorable animal I have never come across.

This remarkable beast lived free in our garden, where it was usually to be found reposing beneath the bushes like one of the lions in front of the New York Public Library with an expression of utmost dignity and calm on its horselike face. At our approach it would merely turn its head, but if called it would arise with tremendous pomposity and proceed towards us with measured tread. Alma was her highness's first love for she brought roasted peanuts which the capybara accepted haughtily, picking them gently and daintily two by two from Alma's hand with her lips, just as a horse might do. Never ruffled, never hurried, this stately creature would proceed about dinnertime to our table, where she would stand serenely and utter the tiniest plaintive whistling squeak. This seemed to indicate slight annoyance, for until food was put before her she steadfastly refused to leave.

On one occasion she chose to leave our grounds. There was nothing in this action that might be construed as running away, for after a leisurely parade through the main streets of Paramaribo she visited the military barracks and apparently decided that the quality of the grass and the traditional air of the place suited her. Next day she returned with a string round her neck, attached at the other end to a corporal in uniform. Such is the dignity of the beast, that it would put our pampered smelly hounds to shame. I dote upon the picture of her proceeding sedately through Hyde Park in a blue felt coat on a bright spring morning, or gracing the Sunday morning parade in the Bois de Boulogne with her presence. Her appearance would startle people but there could be little complaint, for her hard red coat is always immaculately clean.

Persecuted Furbearers

The hundreds of rodent species found in South America have been classified into 16 families, 11 of which are unique to that continent. Many of these creatures have shy, wary natures and live in jungle or mountain habitats, which make them difficult to observe in the wild, and therefore little is known of them. However, numerous South American rodents are plentiful within their geographic ranges and have become familiar to man as quarry.

Agoutis, for example, are hunted for their meat. As a result, these normally diurnal herbivores have become nocturnal in the areas where they are threatened.

Among the most famous South American rodents are the chinchillas, whose soft, silky fur is known and coveted as a luxury all over the world. Chinchillas have been preyed upon so heavily for their pelts that they are virtually extinct in the wild. The bristly pelage of the spiny rat, on the other hand, is of no value to man. Spiny rats are often seen lacking fractions of their tails, which break off easily. Called autotomy, this characteristic reflex aids the spiny rat in escaping from a predator that has caught it by the tail.

A female chinchilla and her youngster huddle in a rocky crevice (above). Sociable creatures in the wild, colonies of chinchillas once inhabited the slopes of the Andes. Today they are found almost exclusively on breeding farms.

A spiny rat grasps a Brazil nut firmly in its incisors. Usually found in crevices beneath the roots of trees or in rocks, most of these rodents come out after dusk to forage for a wide variety of vegetation, including leaves, grasses, fruits and nuts.

A quartet of agoutis (left) scours a grassy patch of countryside looking for leaves, fruit, nuts and roots. Agoutis sit up on their hind legs as they eat, holding food in their forepaws. If threatened, they are able to make a hasty retreat from this position.

Rodents with a Difference

For a number of reasons, the mara, or Patagonian cavy, is a somewhat unconventional rodent. Its long legs, prominent ears and diminutive tail make it look more like a rabbit or a hare than like any other rodent. And when it basks in the warmth of the South American sun, a favorite pastime, the mara either lies on its stomach with its front legs fully extended or it sprawls on its side with all four legs outstretched, a recumbent position far more like that of a cat or dog than of a rodent.

Maras frequent the arid and rocky expanses of the Argentinean pampas and Patagonia, where they inhabit burrows that they either dig themselves or appropriate after the holes have been excavated by other animals.

Maras' forefeet have four digits each that bear sharp claws. Their long hind legs are furnished with three digits and blunt claws suited to running or stotting—the mara's rapid bounding gait, in which all four legs come off the ground at the same time. Stotting maras can reach velocities of up to 18 mph. Their sudden bursts of speed—usually exhibited in times of danger—and the sight of their white rump patches bobbing across country send a warning signal to other maras nearby.

A group of maras, including adults and young (above), loll in the sun not far from the entrance to their communal burrow. Maras are active during the daylight hours, when they feed on roots, stems and grasses. At night they retire to their burrows.

A female mara (right) sits as her two youngsters grope through her fur in an effort to nurse. Maras give birth to two litters of from two to five cubs each year. Females sit on their haunches rather than recline when they nurse—forcing their young to adopt the same alert posture.

The coypu's long orange incisors, a dominant facial characteristic (left), are just one of its distinguishing features. Another is its cylindrical tail, which grows up to 18 inches long. Coypus have webbed hind feet and unwebbed forefeet tipped with powerful claws.

A Water Lover

A strong and skillful swimmer—though more often seen lazily paddling about in search of aquatic plants floating on the water's surface—the coypu is a two-foot-long, 20-pound native of the southern and central parts of South America that loves the water but lives primarily in burrows on land. Coypus are generally found along the banks of rivers and other inland bodies of water. They dig their own burrows or, if there are no suitable sites for burrows, build nests from vegetation that they find along the shore or in shallow water.

Coypus have no fixed breeding period. Females can give birth throughout the year to two litters of as many as five to eight young after a 120- to 132-day gestation period. When they are a day or two old, coypus begin swimming and taking solid food, and at the age of only two weeks they are able to survive without their mothers.

Like chinchillas, coypus have been hunted extensively for their flesh and thick, soft, velvety underfur, which is called nutria by commercial furriers. The coypu population has diminished so dramatically over the years that it is now a protected species in Argentina and in other parts of South America.

A coypu watches as an oblivious duck drifts by. The rodent is merely an onlooker, posing no actual threat to the bird; coypus feed almost exclusively on aquatic plants. Some coypus, however, have been known to sample mollusks.

Porcupines

Campers in the forests of North America know the porcupine well—an animated quiver of quills that waddles slowly down mountain trails, climbs trees with the surefootedness if not the acrobatic insouciance of a monkey, and chews ax handles and boots redolent of human sweat in an attempt to satisfy its virtually insatiable appetite for salt. Porcupines (the name derives from the Latin *porcus* and the French *épin*, meaning "quilled pig") are divided into two families—the Old World porcupines, which are found in Africa and Asia, and the New World porcupines, which range throughout North and South America. The Old World species are chiefly terrestrial while the New World types lead primarily arboreal lives. Wherever it lives, the porcupine is a rodent with a formidable defense system. There are, to be sure, other animals that have evolved spiny quills as a means of protection—the hedgehog of Europe, an insectivore, and the strange, egg-laying echidna, or spiny anteater of Australia—but not one has developed a bristling arsenal to equal the porcupine's. "To specialize and grow quills," wrote naturalist Ernest Thompson Seton, "[the porcupine] has relinquished speed, cunning and keenness of senses; all the revenues of its body seem to have been converted to the growing of these awful spines."

The porcupine's quills are modified hairs tipped with tiny barbs that expand and work their way inward when they encounter the warm flesh and blood of a victim. The porcupine has three different types of pelage: short brown inner fur, quills, and light-brown guard hairs that cover the quills in winter. The guard hairs molt in summer, but the quills grow continuously until they are shed and replaced by new quills.

Legends have grown up about these quills. They are not missiles—the porcupine is unable to project them into the air at an enemy, as old wives' tales have it. But when the quills are erect in a defensive position, they detach easily from the porcupine's body and can penetrate an attacker's flesh like tiny stilettos. Although the porcupine's breeding habits in the wild have not been scientifically documented, the quills may make it necessary for them to mate in a rather gingerly fashion. One study of a captive pair of mating porcupines observed the female on four feet and the male standing erect behind her, using his tail and hind legs for support, and taking care not to embrace her bristling back.

Rightly do these quills command respect, for they are potentially lethal. A swipe of a porcupine's tail across the muzzle of a panther or a wolf can result in a slow and painful death for the predator: Helpless to pull out the quills and unable to eat as they work their way into its mouth and throat, the wretched animal starves to death. More often, however, the offending barbs gradually work their way out of the flesh.

One animal, the quick and graceful fisher, a large member of the weasel family, is the porcupine's nemesis. A fisher can almost always kill a porcupine by attacking its vulnerable snout and face. The fisher finishes the attack by rolling the porcupine over on its back and makes a meal of its sparsely barbed underside. In similar fashion, wolverines of northern woods are often able to get the better of porcupines. Other animals, however, will take on the needly creatures only when starving. Since fishers, wolverines and desperate predators are all rare, porcupines fear few enemies.

As with everything else they do, porcupines are slow to breed. A female North American porcupine produces just one offspring a year, while the South American porcupine's litter consists of four young. The gestation period, 209 days, is extraordinarily long for a rodent. (House mice, by contrast, reproduce in just three weeks and may give birth to as many as 12 litters a year, with four to seven young a litter.) Newborn porcupines are self-sufficient, and their quills are completely hardened a few hours after birth. They are able to climb and eat leaves within a few days. The quills become hollow as the porcupettes grow, giving the animals added buoyancy and enabling them to swim as well as they climb. Mostly nocturnal, the spiny creatures come out to feed at dusk and dawn and by the light of the moon, spending their days dozing in the branches of trees.

South American tree porcupines, or coendous, are armed with shorter, smaller quills and spend most of their time in trees. Coendous are equipped with prehensile tails that enable them to swing like monkeys and to get around with much more agility than their North American brethren. The crested porcupine of tropical Africa is the largest of the spiny animals, growing to a length of over three feet. It is also the most arrogant of the family, and when it is threatened, it will charge any intruder—running backward, exposing its heavily quilled hindquarters as a warning and rattling its formidable one-foot-long quills like a bunch of sabers.

A South American prehensile-tailed porcupine waddles across a fallen log (above), and another maneuvers agilely at the top of a tree (right), its tail wrapped around a branch for security. This arboreal species of porcupine likes to sleep in a mass of tangled vegetation in a treetop.

Bristling Weaponry

The porcupine is one of the world's most placid animals. Slow-moving, it relies upon its excellent defense system of sharp-tipped quills to ward off molesters, and when food is abundant, it is the rare predator that will even attempt to attack the prickly creature.

In the spring, Old World porcupines have litters of one to four cubs, or porcupettes, but the North American porcupines produce only a single cub. Porcupettes can be up to 12 inches long at birth—larger than a bear cub. The young are born fully quilled, but these spines stay soft while the cub is in the womb and do not harden until shortly after birth, when they dry. Although porcupettes may remain with their mothers for several months, they can survive on their own at a much earlier age, subsisting on the bark and leaves they begin eating when only two weeks old.

Porcupines will eat many kinds of vegetation and will even sample dead birds and animals. Their powerful teeth and jaws are superbly adapted for gnawing and grinding. Even northern species of porcupines do not hibernate. They are able to survive in winter by gnawing off the bark of trees to get at the sap-sweet layers underneath.

Using its specially adapted claws and toes, a North American porcupine clings to the slender branches at the the top of a tree (above). The second largest rodent in North America—beavers are bigger—this porcupine eats the needles as well as the bark of evergreen trees.

A North American porcupine (opposite) sniffs the ground in search of something to eat. Porcupines have only fair eyesight and must identify food, intruding animals and potential mates by smell, a more highly developed sense.

The barb-tipped quills of the North American porcupine (below) give it its scientific name, Erethizon dorsatum, which loosely translated means "irritable back." A porcupine usually turns its back to danger. If this warning posture goes unheeded, the threatened porcupine lashes out with its tail.

An African crested porcupine (above) defensively raises the white plume of bristles on its forehead and the quills on its back. These quills (below) are distinctively banded in black and white. Porcupines can have as many as 30,000 loosely attached quills, each capable of dislodging and sticking into an attacker on contact.

Sloths and Armadillos

Sloths spend much of their time hanging upside down in trees; in their bony shells, armadillos live on open ground. Notwithstanding these dissimilarities, both sloths and armadillos are members of the same 65-million-year-old order of animals that evolved in South America. The name of the order, Edentata, which means toothless, is misleading since only the anteater—another member of this order—is totally toothless and must get its meals solely with its sticky tongue. However, sloths and armadillos, although they have numerous teeth, are without incisors and canines. This lack has little effect on their ability to eat: The sloth subsists on leaves and fruits, and the armadillo will eat anything from plants to snakes.

The slow-moving sloths, which live only in the tropics, are strange-looking creatures with arms much longer than their legs and small, round heads with low foreheads, snub noses and unnoticeable ears. Their bodies are covered with a thick coat of long, coarse, unkempt hair. This coat is often tinged with green from the algae that live among the hairs. These tiny plants provide their hosts with an effective camouflage in the leafy trees they frequent. Apart from such strange adaptations, what makes these lethargic creatures especially interesting is their inverted way of life. Sloths eat, sleep and mate upside down. Females even give birth upside down, usually to a single baby. Sloths are so totally adapted to their turned-over existence that they have difficulty standing. On the rare occasions when a sloth descends from its arboreal home to the ground, it looks like a wounded animal as it drags its body along by its arms, getting a clawhold on something in front of it and pulling itself forward. Hanging upside down, however, requires little effort on the part of the sloth because both hands and feet are equipped with long, curved claws that give it a secure grip. Indeed, the grip is so sure fore and aft that sloths can remain hanging from a branch after they die.

There are two types of sloths, distinguished by the number of their fingers on each hand, which have been commonly and mistakenly called toes. Thus there is a two-toed sloth and a three-toed sloth; one has two fingers and the other has three, but both have the same number of digits on each foot—three. Both are often referred to as tree sloths, in deference to an extinct close relative, the elephant-size ground sloth.

With the lowest body temperatures (ranging from 84° to 94° F.) of any mammal and a metabolic rate lower than most other mammals, sloths are truly torpid, sleeping up to 17 hours a day. When they do move, in a deliberate hand-over-hand fashion, they inch along at an estimated one third of a mile an hour. And they do everything else at a decelerated pace: They digest food slowly, contract their muscles slowly—they even sneeze slowly. However, this sluggishness does have an advantage. Their immobilized, upside-down posture in treetops places them out of sight and reach of many would-be predators.

While sloths seem to have survived by sheer unobtrusiveness, that other group of prehistoric-looking edentates, the armadillos, has lasted by means of a portable defense: a shell of bony plates that shields the head and body and inspired its Spanish name, which means "little armored creature." With the exception of the 40-inch-long giant armadillo, most armadillos are small animals with a maximum size of about two feet. From the southern tip of Argentina to Central America, they are fairly common foragers on the open pampas, meadows and upland plateaus. Only one species, the nine-banded armadillo, has ventured north into the United States.

Despite their rigid appearance, most armadillos are fairly agile. The series of bands in the midsection of their armor is separated by flexible skin that allows them to move their bodies easily. And although their heads, tails and legs are usually covered by bony plates, their underbellies are soft and furry. They trot at a surprising speed, and even with their heavy shells, are able to ford a stream. By swallowing enough air to inflate their digestive tract, they can swim without sinking, and if a stream is not very wide, they simply hold their breath and walk across the bottom.

When armadillos need their shells for protection, they tuck in their head and feet and rest the bottom edge of their armor on the ground. Some, however, can curl themselves up; the three-banded armadillo can roll itself into a cantaloupe-size ball that only a strong-jawed carnivore like a jaguar can crack. Such tactics are generally employed only as a last resort. Armadillos usually escape danger by rapidly digging an underground retreat with their powerful claws. This burrowing ability is especially necessary for the smallest member of the family, the six-inch fairy armadillo, which has an incomplete set of plates on its back but does have a bony shield on its flat rump. When frightened, it bolts into a burrow and blocks the entrance like a cork plugging a bottle.

Three-toed sloths

Armor-plated — But Vulnerable

The nine-banded armadillo is the commonest member of the family of armored edentates, with a range stretching from Argentina to the southern United States. It may venture even farther north if the climate is suitably warm. Though hardy and prolific, and mainly active at night, this 15-inch armadillo is not as invulnerable as it appears. The prey of wolves, coyotes and bobcats, which can easily turn it over and attack its furry belly, it must rely largely on the safety of a burrow when threatened, not on its armor. To increase its chances of taking such shelter, the nine-banded armadillo often builds several burrows in addition to a roomy home base, which may be as long as 15 feet and which will contain a nest of grassy vegetation that the armadillo has collected and kicked into the excavation. However, if it is surprised by a predator at a distance from its retreats, it can improvise in an instant, cutting through hard-packed earth with its razor-sharp claws and burying itself almost out of sight.

Nine-banded armadillos sometimes share a burrow with others of their species, usually of the same sex. And when armadillo babies are born after a once-a-year mating and a 120-day gestation, they are not only quadruplets but—truly identical—they are either all male or all female.

Rooting around in the Texas scrub, a nine-banded armadillo (below) forages for insects. The shell that protects its body consists of an underlayer of bony disks that are covered by outer bands of horny skin.

A three-toed sloth (left) hangs from a tree while slowly changing position. The three-toed sloth is a specialized feeder, almost exclusively eating the leaves of the mulberry-like cecropia tree. At right, a three-toed sloth does the breaststroke across a stretch of the Amazon River. Sloths are more adept in the water than on the ground and have been reported swimming as far as 100 feet.

Slothful Ways

Though sloths are slow animals, their sedentary ways are combined with physical traits that endow them with toughness and endurance. Muscle accounts for only 25 percent of the body weight of both the nine-pound three-toed sloth and the 20-pound two-toed sloth—a percentage that is only half the muscle proportion of most mammals. Yet sloths' forearms are powerful and their claws are sharp and strong. Their long, thick fur serves as insulation and grows toward the head, unlike that of other mammals. This adaptation allows rain to run off when they are hanging upside down. Sloths are dependent on their sense of smell, and they are able to swivel their heads in a 270° arc when sniffing their way through the trees in search of food.

Usually placid and solitary, sloths can become ferocious when defending themselves, biting with sharp teeth, slashing with hooklike claws and inflicting deep wounds on their attackers. However, sloths themselves seem to survive even the severest injuries, and have a life-span that is estimated at about 10 years.

Securely hooked upside down on a limb, a two-toed sloth (overleaf) keeps a hand free for reaching food. The two-toed sloth is not as restricted in its diet as the three-toed and it eats a variety of leaves and fruit, pulling them into its mouth with its long curved claws.

Credits

Cover—H. Silvestre, Photo Researchers, Inc. 1—J. Nagel, Bruce Coleman, Inc. 5—H. Silvestre, P.R., Inc. 6–7—B. & C. Calhoun, B.C., Inc. 17—K. W. Fink, P.R., Inc. 18–19—Tom Brakefield. 19—F. Current, P.R., Inc. 20—Tom Brakefield, Animals Animals. 21—Tom Brakefield, B.C., Inc. 22–23—J. Burton, B.C., Inc. 23 (top)—S. Dalton, P.R., Inc.; (bottom)—G. Meszaros, B.C., Inc. 24—M. Fogden, B.C., Inc. 25 (top)—L. L. Rue, P.R., Inc.; (bottom)—L. Ditto, B.C., Inc. 26–27—Stouffer Productions, Animals Animals. 27 (top)—C. Ott, P.R., Inc.; (bottom)—M. Grosnick, B.C., Inc. 28–29—Tom Brakefield. 32 (top)—Animals Animals; (bottom)—W. Grosnick, B.C., Inc. 33—J. Foott, B.C., Inc. 35—G. Liesler, P.R., Inc. 36—L. L. Rue. 37 (top)—L. L. Rue, P.R., Inc.; (bottom)—L. L. Rue, P.R., Inc. 38–39—P. Caulfield, P.R., Inc. 39 (top)—K. Dean, P.R., Inc.; (bottom)—C. Lockwood, Animals Animals. 41—N. Smythe, P.R., Inc. 42 (bottom)—R. Kinne, P.R., Inc. 42–43—J. Blossom, P.R., Inc. 43—Stouffer Productions, Animals Animals. 44–45—Bruce Coleman, Inc. 45 (top)—J. Couffer, B.C., Inc.; (bottom)—Tom Brakefield. 46—L. Chace, P.R., Inc. 47 (top)—M. Mendez, Animals Animals; (center)—R. Carr, B.C., Inc.; (bottom)—Dr. Degginger, B.C., Inc. 48–49—J. Burton, B.C., Inc. 49 (top)—Bruce Coleman, B.C., Inc.; (bottom)—J. Burton, B.C., Inc. 50 (top)—H. Reinhard, B.C., Inc.; (bottom)—J. Burton, B.C., Inc. 50–51—H. Reinhard, B.C., Inc. 53—S. Bisserot, B.C., Inc. 54–55—Stouffer Productions, Animals Animals. 55—Stouffer Productions, Animals Animals. 56—Bruce Coleman, Inc. 57—G. Harrison, B.C., Inc. 58—W. Bayer. 58–59—W. Bayer. 59 (top)—T. McHugh, P.R., Inc.; (bottom right)—T. McHugh, P.R., Inc. 61—P. Dotson, P.R., Inc. 62—A. Blank, B.C., Inc. 63—Oxford Scientific Films, B.C., Inc. 64 (left)—P. Hay, P.R., Inc.; (right)—L. Wanlass, P.R., Inc. 64–65—J. Burton, B.C., Inc. 65 (top)—J. & D. Bartlett, B.C., Inc. 66 (top)—Tom Brakefield; (bottom)—K. Brate, P.R., Inc. 67—Tom Brakefield. 68 (top left)—P. Ward, B.C., Inc.; (bottom left)—F. Roberts, Animals Animals; (bottom right)—T. McHugh, Chicago Zoo Park, P.R., Inc. 68–69—K. Maslowski, P.R., Inc. 69 (bottom left)—P. Ward, B.C., Inc.; (top right)—T. McHugh, P.R., Inc.; (bottom right)—S. Dalton, P.R., Inc. 72—Z. Leszczynski, Animals Animals. 73—Z. Leszczynski, Animals Animals. 74—J. Markham, B.C., Inc. 75 (top)—J. Markham, B.C., Inc.; (bottom)—T. McHugh, P.R., Inc. 81—F. Grehan, P.R., Inc. 82 (top)—H. Silvestre, P.R., Inc. 82–83—H. Silvestre, P.R., Inc. 83 (top)—H. Silvestre, P.R., Inc. 84—L. L. Rue III, B.C., Inc. 85—L. L. Rue III, B.C., Inc. 88 (top)—P. Miller, P.R., Inc.; (bottom)—George Silk. 88–89—N. Hamilton, P.R., Inc. 90–91—Stouffer Productions, Animals Animals. 92—R. Whitehead, P.R., Inc. 93—J. & D. Bartlett, B.C., Inc. 95—Tom Brakefield. 96–97—Entheos. 97 (top)—Z. Gaal, P.R., Inc.; (bottom)—Z. Gaal, P.R., Inc. 99—S. Lindblad, P.R., Inc. 100–101—K. Weidmann, P.R., Inc. 101—G. Schaller, B.C., Inc. 102—S. Lindblad, P.R., Inc. 106—R. Kinne, P.R., Inc., 107 (top)—D. Houston, B.C., Inc.; (bottom)—J. Burton, B.C., Inc. 108–109—F. Erize, B.C., Inc. 109—D. Bartlett, B.C., Inc. 110—R. Kinne, P.R., Inc. 110–111—T. McHugh, P.R., Inc. 113—Tom Brakefield. 114 (top)—P. Caulfield, P.R., Inc.; (bottom)—R. Kinne, P.R., Inc. 115—B. Mays, P.R., Inc. 116—S. Krasemann, P.R., Inc. 117 (top)—P. R. Thompson and G. D. Dodge, B.C., Inc.; (bottom left)—S. Krasemann, P.R., Inc. 119—S. Wayman, P.R., Inc. 120—N. Proctor, P.R., Inc. 121—H. Hoffman, P.R., Inc. 122—W. Bayer. 123—W. Bayer, 124–125—F. Erize, B.C., Inc.

The photographs on the endpapers are used courtesy of Time-Life Picture Agency and Russ Kinne and Stephen Dalton of Photo Researchers, Inc., and Nina Leen.

The film sequence on page 8 is from "Animals of the Avalanche," a program in the Time-Life Television series *Wild, Wild World of Animals*.

ILLUSTRATIONS on pages 9 and 14 courtesy of The Bettmann Archive. The illustration on pages 10–11 by Beatrix Potter, © Frederick Warne & Co., N.Y. & London, courtesy of Frederick Warne & Co. The illustration on page 12 is by Gustave Doré. The illustration on page 15 is by Garth Williams, from *Stuart Little* by E. B. White, copyright 1945 by E. B. White, illustration copyright renewed © 1973 by Garth Williams, reprinted by permission of the publishers, Harper & Row, Inc. The illustrations on pages 30–31 are by Charles Robinson, those on pages 70–71 by Charles B. Slackman, those on pages 77–79 by John Groth, those on pages 86–87 by André Durenceau, that on page 105 by Jerry Gersten.

Bibliography

NOTE: An asterisk at the left means that a paperback volume is also available.

Anderson, Sydney, ed., *Recent Mammals of the World*. The Ronald Press Company, 1967.

Bailey, Vernon, *Mammals of the Southwestern United States*. Dover Publications, 1971.

Boulière, François, *The Natural History of Mammals*. Alfred A. Knopf, 1964.

Caras, Roger, *North American Mammals*. Meredith Press, 1967.

Corbet, G. B., *The Terrestrial Mammals of Western Europe*. Dufour Editions, 1966.

Dorst, Jean, and Pierre Dandelot, *A Field Guide to the Larger Mammals of Africa*. Collins, 1970.

Godin, Alfred J., *Wild Mammals of New England*. Johns Hopkins University Press, 1977.

Hoffmeister, Donald F., *Mammals of Grand Canyon*. University of Illinois Press, 1971.

Jackson, Hartley H. T., *Mammals of Wisconsin*. University of Wisconsin Press, 1961.

Lane, C. H., *Rabbits, Cats and Cavies*. E. P. Dutton, 1903.

*Lockley, Robert Mathias, *The Private Life of the Rabbit*. Macmillan, 1974.

Matthews, L. Harrison, *The Life of Mammals*, vols. 1 and 2. Universe Books, 1969, 1971.

Medway, Lord:
  Mammals of Borneo. Malaysian Branch of the Royal Asiatic Society, 1965.
  The Wild Mammals of Malaya. Oxford University Press, 1969.

Orr, Robert T., *The Little-known Pika*. Macmillan, 1977.

Peterson, Randolph L., *The Mammals of Eastern Canada*. Oxford University Press, 1966.

Rosevear, D. R., *The Rodents of Western Africa*. Trustees of the British Museum (Natural History), 1969.

Sanderson, Ivan T., *Living Mammals of the World*. Hanover House, 1955.

Schoonmaker, W. J., *The World of the Woodchuck*. J. B. Lippincott, 1966.

Schultz, Adolph H., *The Life of Primates*. Universe Books, 1969.

Schwartz, Charles W. and Elizabeth R., *The Wild Animals of Missouri*. University of Missouri Press, 1959.

Smithers, Reay H. N., *The Mammals of Botswana*. The Trustees of the National Museums of Rhodesia, 1971.

Southern, H. N., *The Handbook of British Mammals*. Blackwell Scientific Publications, 1964.

Walker, Ernest P., *Mammals of the World*. Johns Hopkins University Press, 1975.